Remuneration of Boards of Directors and Executive Management in State-Owned Enterprises

I0024745

OECD

BETTER POLICIES FOR BETTER LIVES

This document, as well as any data and map included herein, are without prejudice to the status of or sovereignty over any territory, to the delimitation of international frontiers and boundaries and to the name of any territory, city or area.

The statistical data for Israel are supplied by and under the responsibility of the relevant Israeli authorities. The use of such data by the OECD is without prejudice to the status of the Golan Heights, East Jerusalem and Israeli settlements in the West Bank under the terms of international law.

Note by Turkey
The information in this document with reference to "Cyprus" relates to the southern part of the Island. There is no single authority representing both Turkish and Greek Cypriot people on the Island. Turkey recognises the Turkish Republic of Northern Cyprus (TRNC). Until a lasting and equitable solution is found within the context of the United Nations, Turkey shall preserve its position concerning the "Cyprus issue".

Note by all the European Union Member States of the OECD and the European Union
The Republic of Cyprus is recognised by all members of the United Nations with the exception of Turkey. The information in this document relates to the area under the effective control of the Government of the Republic of Cyprus.

Please cite this publication as:
OECD (2022), *Remuneration of Boards of Directors and Executive Management in State-Owned Enterprises*, OECD Publishing, Paris, https://doi.org/10.1787/80d6dc04-en.

ISBN 978-92-64-86380-4 (print)
ISBN 978-92-64-35932-1 (pdf)
ISBN 978-92-64-39859-7 (HTML)
ISBN 978-92-64-65415-0 (epub)

Photo credits: Cover © bluejayphoto/Getty Images.

Corrigenda to publications may be found on line at: www.oecd.org/about/publishing/corrigenda.htm.
© OECD 2022

The use of this work, whether digital or print, is governed by the Terms and Conditions to be found at https://www.oecd.org/termsandconditions.

Foreword

The remuneration of board members and key executives of listed companies has received considerable attention in the past decade. By contrast, the same issue has yet to be fully addressed in the case of state-owned enterprises (SOEs). This report seeks to fill the gap by taking stock of the policies and practices underpinning the remuneration of supervisory board members and executive managers of SOEs across 36 OECD member and partner countries.

The report focuses on provisions applicable to supervisory board members (or non-executive directors, in the case of one-tier boards) and executive managers (or executive directors) of unlisted and majority-owned SOEs with more than 50% of state shareholding. Information was collected through a questionnaire – and supplemented by desk research – from 36 countries: Australia, Austria, Belgium, Brazil, Bulgaria, Chile, Colombia, Costa Rica, Croatia, the Czech Republic, Estonia, Finland, France, Germany, Greece, Hungary, Iceland, Ireland, Israel, Japan, Korea, Latvia, Lithuania, Mexico, the Netherlands, New Zealand, Norway, Peru, Philippines, Portugal, the Slovak Republic, Spain, Sweden, Switzerland, Turkey and the United Kingdom.

This stocktaking report was developed under the auspices of the OECD Working Party on State Ownership and Privatisation Practices to provide:

- A comprehensive mapping of the remuneration policies and practices of governing bodies of SOEs in OECD member and partner countries, assessing actual practices against the recommendations laid down in the *OECD Guidelines on Corporate Governance of State-Owned Enterprises*.

- A guidepost for a future revision of the *OECD Guidelines on Corporate Governance of State-Owned Enterprises*.

The report was authored by Emeline Denis, under the supervision of Hans Christiansen, both of the Corporate Governance and Corporate Finance Division of the OECD Directorate for Financial and Enterprise Affairs. It was prepared for publication by Greta Gabbarini and Liv Gudmundson.

Table of contents

Foreword 3

Executive summary 6

1 Setting the scene: rationale, scope and methodology 9
    1.1. Rationale 9
    1.2. Scope 10
    1.3. Methodology 12
    References 12
    Notes 13

2 Remuneration schemes applicable to supervisory board members 15
    2.1. Introduction 15
    2.2. Actual remuneration levels of supervisory board members according to SOE corporate characteristics 18
    2.3. Remuneration policies and practices 23
    2.4. Transparency and disclosure practices 40
    References 42
    Notes 44

3 Remuneration schemes applicable to executive management of SOEs 47
    3.1. Introduction 47
    3.2. Actual remuneration levels of executive managers according to SOE corporate characteristics 49
    3.3. Remuneration policies and practices 52
    3.4. Transparency and disclosure practices 64
    References 68
    Notes 69

Annex A. SOE classification according to orientation and size 71

Annex B. Actual remuneration levels of supervisory board members according SOEs' orientation and size 81

Annex C. Actual remuneration levels of executive managers according to SOEs' orientation and size 87

FIGURES

Figure 2.1. Average annual remuneration of ordinary board members of SOEs (in USD as of 2020) 18
Figure 2.2. Average annual remuneration of ordinary board members of SOEs as a percentage of average annual national wages (as of 2020) 19
Figure 2.3. Comparing remuneration levels of board chairs and ordinary board members of commercially oriented and public policy-oriented SOEs 21
Figure 2.4. How is board remuneration decided? 24
Figure 2.5. Remuneration components 29
Figure 2.6. Can civil servants or other state officials serve on boards? 34
Figure 2.7. Disclosure practices by SOEs and the state regarding board remuneration levels 41
Figure 3.1. Average annual remuneration of CEOs of SOEs (fixed remuneration only, in USD as of 2020) 50
Figure 3.2. Average annual remuneration of CEOs of SOEs (fixed remuneration only, as a multiple of average annual national wages) 51
Figure 3.3. Remuneration policies and practices for executive managers of SOEs 53
Figure 3.4. Performance-related remuneration component of executive managers of SOE 55
Figure 3.5. Relative importance of the various components of the remuneration effectively allocated in 2020 before employer's social contribution 66
Figure 3.6. Disclosure of remuneration levels of executive managers by the government or ownership entity 67

Figure A.1. Indicators and criteria for establishing the total score in public enterprises in Bulgaria 75

TABLES

Table 2.1. Application of the five calculation methods to each SOE in Costa Rica 27
Table 2.2. Types of board remuneration policies 28
Table 2.3. Criteria for setting board remuneration in Colombian SOEs 30
Table 2.4. Remuneration policies and practices of supervisory board members across 36 jurisdictions 35
Table 3.1. Selected approaches for capping performance-related compensation of executives of SOEs 55
Table 3.2. Eligibility criteria for performance-based compensation in the Philippine 57
Table 3.3. Remuneration policies and practices for executive managers of SOEs across 34 jurisdictions 58
Table 3.4. Remuneration overview of the CEO 65
Table 3.5. Remuneration overview of the other members of the Executive Committee 65

Table A A.1. Fees payable to chairpersons and members of state bodies in Ireland 76
Table A A.2. Remuneration levels of non-executive directors of SOEs in Portugal 78
Table A A.3. Remuneration levels of executive managers of SOEs in Portugal 78
Table A A.4. Classification of GOCC according to their total amount of assets and revenues 79
Table A A.5. Maximum allowable allowances per meeting and per year (according to GOCC classification) 79
Table A A.6. Actual annual average remuneration of an individual board member (according to GOCC classification) 79
Table A B.1. Average annual remuneration of supervisory board members of commercially oriented SOEs 81
Table A B.2. Average annual remuneration of supervisory board members of public policy-oriented SOEs 84
Table A C.1. Average annual remuneration of executive managers of commercially oriented SOEs (in actual USD and as a multiple of average wages) 87
Table A C.2. Average annual remuneration of executive managers of public policy-oriented SOEs (in actual USD and as a multiple of average wages) 89

Executive summary

The remuneration of boards and executive management presents concrete challenges for the ownership of SOEs, and it straddles the spheres of corporate and public sector governance. While remuneration schemes falling below market levels may hamper the recruitment of qualified candidates, remuneration levels perceived as being too high can cause a public backlash. This issue also bears relevance in the midst of the COVID-19 crisis, which has increased scrutiny of executive pay packages and may be an opportunity to reconsider executive pay generally to "build back better".

Recognising the importance of devising adequate remuneration schemes for the board and executive members of SOEs, this report takes stock of the policies and practices underpinning the remuneration of governing bodies of SOEs across 36 OECD member and partner countries. Its main findings can be summarised as follows.

Remuneration schemes applicable to supervisory board members of SOEs

While board remuneration levels are formally approved by the AGM in almost all countries, in practice different procedures exist across countries for setting the amounts of board fees. In countries with mainly commercial SOEs, remuneration seems to either be proposed by the remuneration committees of SOEs or set by the central ownership unit based on private sector benchmarks. By contrast, in countries with policy-oriented SOEs – including those operating under monopoly situations, or with a majority of SOEs of "strategic interest", remuneration tends to either be set by law or based on public sector wage grids. Such measures were also introduced in countries severely impacted by the 2008 global financial crisis, and have remained in place for the past decade. Some countries also report different procedures according to the corporate form, share of state ownership and listing status of SOEs.

While remuneration levels can vary according to the size of SOEs and their sector of operation, on average, board members of commercially oriented SOEs tend to receive higher fees than those of public policy-oriented SOEs. Overall however, aggregate SOE board remuneration levels seem to stand significantly below those of private companies, which has reportedly hampered the recruitment of competent board members in several countries. Some countries do, however, perceive a vocational element of service to the public interest as a key lever for competent professionals to consider a board position within an SOE, as this may be associated either with prestige or with the fulfilment of a public duty.

There are considerable national differences to the basis by which board members are remunerated across countries. Board members may receive fixed fees, board meeting allowances, or a combination or both, which may be supplemented by additional fees for the membership of board committees. Allowances that cover actual costs related to the board duties, including travelling, are added in some cases. Other forms of remuneration such as short-term bonuses and performance-related compensation are generally not granted to supervisory board members, reportedly to avoid fears that it may compromise their independence by encouraging management to take excessive short-term risks.

Remunerated civil servants on boards can also give rise to potential conflicts of interest, as this may incentivise them to take an excessive number of directorships and to seek board membership in companies with the highest remuneration practices. As such, in many countries where civil servants are allowed to serve on boards and receive compensation, provisions have been introduced to limit the number of board seats that they may fill, as well as to cap their remuneration and to treat them like other independent members with regard to their selection, responsibilities and liabilities.

Remuneration schemes applicable to executive management of SOEs

Practices regarding executive remuneration vary significantly across countries. In countries facing specific political or fiscal constraints, remuneration is generally prescribed by law or by separate government decision, with levels standing (sometimes significantly) below the average of SOEs in other countries and lower than market levels in the domestic economy. On the other hand, in countries where remuneration is set at the full discretion of the board, levels are generally higher – sometimes explicitly based on private sector benchmarks.

Average CEO remuneration in commercially oriented SOEs is double that of public policy-oriented SOEs, except in countries where levels are set by law. In many countries, the disparity between remuneration levels of CEOs of large SOEs and small SOEs is also significant. Some outliers exist by sector, such as the air transport sector, where caps may have been derogated to accommodate generally high sectoral pay levels. Unsurprisingly, the remuneration of the CEO is generally higher than the remuneration of other executive managers. In some cases, the differences actually seem to be smaller than may be expected in the private sector. Executive managers are mostly hired on fixed-term contracts rather than on continuous contracts with terms for termination found in the private sector in a number of countries.

Pay packages of executive managers usually include an annual fixed salary, allowances, fringe benefits and payments to the pension plan, and can also include severance payments. Stock options are generally not allowed. In almost all countries, executive managers' pay packages also include a performance-based component. The latter, in turn, is capped by the government owner in more than half of surveyed countries, mostly at a percentage of the fixed remuneration component rather than at the absolute level. While limited information is available regarding how performance is benchmarked since these key performance indicators are mostly set at the full discretion of the board and not by government – and thus vary across companies, many countries mention that performance is benchmarked against profitability relative to other companies and compared to the previous year.

In almost all countries, SOEs are required to disclose information on the remuneration levels of executive managers to the general public, along with the remuneration policy including details of the bonus schemes in many countries. In some countries, disclosure requirements apply only to the remuneration of the CEO and/or only in the case of listed companies. Interestingly, some countries which have faced controversy over high executive remuneration have strengthened their disclosure requirements in recent years, in an effort to align them with those applicable to listed companies where information of higher granularity is required to be disclosed. By contrast, the state or ownership entity discloses information on executive remuneration in only around half of the surveyed countries, mainly through a central government portal, or the government or ownership entity's annual report on SOEs.

1 Setting the scene: rationale, scope and methodology

This chapter sets out the context for undertaking this study, and underlines the main issues with regard to board and executive remuneration in state-owned enterprises (SOEs). The chapter then describes the scope of the study, and its underlying methodology.

1.1. Rationale

The governance of the remuneration of board members and key executives of listed companies has received considerable attention in the past decade.[1] By contrast, the issue of executive and board remuneration of SOEs has to date apparently not been addressed in detail by other international organisations and standard-setting bodies. While this report fills an important gap, it is also aiming to assess the degree to which SOE practices coincide with, or depart from, the practices in listed companies.[2]

Overall, the remuneration of boards and executive management presents concrete challenges for the ownership of SOEs. While remuneration schemes for SOE board and executive members should reflect market conditions to the extent that this is necessary to attract and retain qualified directors and executives, in practice it seems that remuneration in many OECD countries falls below market levels. This reflects *inter alia* the fact that governments seek to avoid public controversy over excessive pay in the public sector. A further concern is that the excessive remuneration of underperforming SOEs provides the wrong incentives for executive and board members, and hence can lead to inefficiencies and a lack of accountability.

In particular, remuneration levels perceived as being too high – especially with regards to variable components of remuneration such as bonuses and/or redundancy payments – can cause a public backlash, especially when these do not seem to reflect the SOEs' performance. For instance, in several OECD countries the remuneration of CEOs of SOEs in the aviation sector has received media attention a few years ago (e.g. in Finland and Latvia), in some cases leading to corrective measures by the state (Reuters, 2018[1]; Baltic Times, 2014[2]; Finnair, 2018[3]). More broad-based controversies have also arisen in some other countries, including in New Zealand, where SOE executives have been alleged to receive high performance bonuses "regardless of how the organisation is doing", and in South Africa, where the media has repeatedly criticised in recent years the remuneration packages and annual bonuses of executive and board members of "loss-making" SOEs that "fail to deliver services" or are "frequently bailed out with public funds" (Stuff, 2018[4]; University of the Witwatersrand, 2020[5]).

As a result, many countries have introduced some limits and restrictions on the remuneration and employment conditions of SOE board and executive members (OECD, 2013[6]). However, such limits can also have adverse effects, as uncompetitive remuneration levels can impact SOEs' ability to attract competent candidates from the private sector, therefore impacting the quality of boards and executive management. In Korea for instance, the remuneration of non-executive directors has risen considerably for the last 10 to 15 years in order to attract more professional candidates (OECD, 2018[7]). In Croatia, SOEs reportedly encounter similar difficulties in hiring members with sectoral experience in view of the poor remuneration of SOE boards as compared to competitors in the private sector (OECD, 2021[8]). Uncompetitive remuneration levels can also limit the pool of qualified candidates by detracting foreigners from considering board membership – a concern raised recently in the case of Ukraine (OECD, 2021[9]).

Recognising the importance of devising adequate remuneration schemes of board and executive members of SOEs, this issue also bears relevance in the midst of the COVID-19 crisis, which has brought executive remuneration (of listed companies in particular) into the spotlight with directors encouraged to "share the pain" of employees and investors by forgoing salary, bonus and share-based awards, particularly where shareholders have had dividend payments cut. While it may be argued that the crisis stands as an opportunity to reconsider executive pay generally in order to "build back better", increasing scrutiny of executive pay packages is also expected in years to come.

1.2. Scope

The subject of board and managerial remuneration is to some extent covered by the OECD's existent SOE-related instruments. While the *OECD Guidelines on Corporate Governance of State-Owned Enterprises* ("SOE Guidelines") state that the remuneration of both SOE boards and executive management should be aligned with the long-term interest of the enterprise, and effectively identify some of the main issues underpinning board and executive remuneration, they offer little advice on how best to address them (Box 1).

> ### Box 1. OECD Guidelines on Corporate Governance of State-Owned Enterprises
>
> #### Board of directors
>
> With regard to the *boards of directors*, the SOE Guidelines posit that "[t]here is a strong case for aligning the remuneration of board members of SOEs with private sector practices. ... However, care should also be taken to effectively manage any potential backlash against SOEs and the ownership entity due to negative public perception triggered by excessive board remuneration levels. This can pose a challenge for attracting top talent to SOE boards, although other factors such as reputational benefits, prestige and access to networking are sometimes considered to represent non-negligible aspects of board remuneration" (annotations to Chapter II point F).
>
> #### Executive management
>
> Concerning the *executive management*, the SOE Guidelines further offer that boards should "decide, subject to applicable rules established by the state, on the compensation of the CEO. They should ensure that the CEO's remuneration is tied to performance and duly disclosed. Compensation packages for senior executives should be competitive, but care should be taken not to incentivise management in a way inconsistent with the long-term interest of the enterprise and its owners. The introduction of malus and claw-back provisions is considered a good practice..." (annotations to Chapter VII, point B). This effectively recommends the inclusion of a performance-related element in executive managers' pay packages.
>
> #### Transparency and disclosure
>
> Finally, on the issue of *transparency and disclosure,* the SOE Guidelines observe that "[i]t is important that SOEs ensure high levels of transparency regarding the remuneration of board members and key executives. Failure to provide adequate information to the public could result in negative perceptions and fuel risks of a backlash against the ownership entity and individual SOEs. Information should relate to actual remuneration levels and the policies that underpin them" (annotations to Chapter VI, Point A). It indicates that it is considered in the interest of ownership entities to opt for maximum transparency, even at the risk of spurring public anger by disclosing pay levels that may be considered as excessive.
>
> Source: OECD (2015[10]), *OECD Guidelines on Corporate Governance of State-Owned Enterprises,* https://www.oecd.org/corporate/guidelines-corporate-governance-soes.htm.

Against this background, this report provides a comprehensive mapping of the remuneration practices in OECD member and partner countries, along with a review of examples of recent and ongoing reform. As such, the report covers (i) direct action and rules implemented by the state as an enterprise owner, (ii) ownership policies, owner's expectations and guidelines issued by the state, and (iii) general laws and regulations bearing on SOE remuneration. While detailed information on remuneration systems is provided for both board and executive members of SOEs, for executive managers in particular, consideration is given to the extent to which the state as an owner influences the board of directors' autonomy to decide on managerial remuneration and incentives.

In terms of coverage, this report focuses on provisions applicable to supervisory board members (or non-executive directors, in the case of one-tier boards) and executive managers (or executive directors) of majority-owned SOEs with more than 50% state shareholding which are not listed on the stock exchange. Overall, the report highlights differences in remuneration practices according to the corporate context, including the size of the SOEs, their commercial and non-commercial orientations, and the sectors in which they operate.[3]

1.3. Methodology

To prepare this report, information was collected through a questionnaire and supplemented by desk research. Overall, 31 OECD member and five partner countries provided responses to the questionnaire: Australia, Austria, Belgium, Brazil, Bulgaria, Chile, Colombia, Costa Rica, Croatia, the Czech Republic, Estonia, Finland, France, Germany, Greece, Hungary, Iceland, Ireland,[4] Israel, Japan, Korea, Latvia, Lithuania, Mexico, the Netherlands, New Zealand, Norway, Peru, Philippines, Portugal, the Slovak Republic, Spain, Sweden, Switzerland, Turkey and the United Kingdom.

It should be noted that some caveats exist regarding the sample size and comprehensiveness of the information collected in some countries. In Australia, information was provided by the Department of Finance, which does not have a direct role in the management and determination of remuneration of SOEs. As such, comprehensive information was not available. In Belgium, information collected covered the four SOEs in the portfolio of the Ministry of Finance only (Skeyes, NMBS/SMCB, Proximus, and Bpost), hence excluding SOEs in the portfolio of the Federal Holding and Investment Company (SFPI-FPIM). In Japan, where a dispersed state ownership structure exists, information was collected on the practices in place in five SOEs (Japan Tabacco, Tokyo Metro Co. Ltd, Hokkaido Railway Company, Shikoky Railway Company, and Japan Freight Railway Company). In the United Kingdom, information provided covers the 13 SOEs in the UKGI portfolio.

Finally, while acknowledging that a given practice can be performed in different ways to a similar effect, the contents of the present report may also be influenced by the individual respondents' choice of wording. Moreover, some of the questions in the questionnaire may not closely reflect all countries' ownership and governance models, in which case the respondents will have picked the answers that they think most closely reflects their national practices.

References

Baltic Times (2014), *Air Baltic CEO salary increases 65 percent*, https://www.baltictimes.com/news/articles/34980/. [2]

BIS (2011), *Range of Methodologies for Risk and Performance Alignment of Remuneration*, https://www.bis.org/publ/bcbs194.pdf. [12]

Finnair (2018), *Remuneration Statement 2018*, https://investors.finnair.com/~/media/Files/F/Finnair-IR/documents/en/governance/remuneration-statement-2018.pdf. [3]

FSB (2009), *FSB Principles for Sound Compensation Practices*, https://www.fsb.org/wp-content/uploads/r_0904b.pdf. [11]

OECD (2021), *OECD Review of the Corporate Governance of State-Owned Enterprises in Croatia*, https://www.oecd.org/corporate/soe-review-croatia.htm#:~:text=The%20OECD%20Review%20of%20Croatia,the%20%E2%80%9CSOE%20Guidelines percentageE2%80%9D). [8]

OECD (2021), *OECD Review of the Corporate Governance of State-Owned Enterprises: Ukraine*, https://www.oecd.org/corporate/soe-review-ukraine.htm. [9]

OECD (2018), *Professionalising Boards of Directors of State-Owned Enterprises: Stocktaking of National Practices*, https://www.oecd.org/corporate/Professionalising-boards-of-directors-of-SOEs.pdf. [7]

OECD (2015), *OECD Guidelines on Corporate Governance of State-Owned Enterprises*, [10]
https://www.oecd.org/corporate/guidelines-corporate-governance-soes.htm.

OECD (2013), *Boards of Directors of State-Owned Enterprises: An Overview of National* [6]
Practices, Corporate Governance, OECD Publishing, Paris,
https://doi.org/10.1787/9789264200425-en.

OECD (2011), *Board Practices: Incentives and Governing Risks*, Corporate Governance, OECD [13]
Publishing, Paris, https://doi.org/10.1787/9789264113534-en.

Reuters (2018), *Finnair board member quits after government lambasts CEO pension*, [1]
https://www.reuters.com/article/uk-finnair-board-government-idUKKBN1FK19Z.

Stuff (2018), *Pay rises for SOE bosses as public service CEOs miss out*, [4]
https://www.stuff.co.nz/business/farming/107758958/stateowned-enterprise-bosses-
dodge-clamp-down-on-pay.

University of the Witwatersrand (2020), *Capping executive pay is the key to stop money-guzzling* [5]
SOEs from ruining SA, https://www.wits.ac.za/news/latest-
news/opinion/2020/2020-10/capping-executive-pay-is-the-key-to-stop-money-guzzling-soes-
from-ruining-sa.html.

Notes

[1] Executive remuneration schemes in listed companies and financial institutions in particular have been subjected to strengthened regulation since the 2008 global financial crisis, including in the European Union and the United States. In addition, in 2009, the Financial Stability Board issued *Principles for Sound Compensation Practices* for large financial institutions, in order to align compensation with prudent risk-taking (FSB, 2009[11]). In 2011, the Basel Committee issued a report on the *Range of Methodologies for Risk and Performance Alignment of Remuneration* analysing the methods used by banks for incorporating risk into bonus pools and individual compensation schemes (BIS, 2011[12]).

[2] In 2011, the OECD Corporate Governance Committee issued a peer review of remuneration and incentives in listed companies, which subsequently served as a basis for revising the *G20/OECD Principles of Corporate Governance* in 2015, as well as for collecting information on how these policies and practices are implemented *inter alia* across all OECD, G20 and Financial Stability Board members in the OECD Corporate Governance Factbook, published every two years since 2015 (OECD, 2011[13]).

[3] Detailed information on the criteria underpinning SOE orientation and size is provided in Annex A.

[4] The questionnaire responses from Ireland do not consider financial institutions in respect of which the state retains a shareholding.

2 Remuneration schemes applicable to supervisory board members

This chapter takes stock of policy approaches underpinning the remuneration of ordinary board members, board chairs and board committee members across countries. The chapter explores the extent to which board remuneration practices and levels relate to countries' ownership arrangements and their SOEs' corporate characteristics – including their size, commercial and non-commercial orientation, and sector of operation. It also takes stock of transparency and disclosure practices by ownership entities and SOEs.

2.1. Introduction

As commonly recognised, boards play a central function in corporate governance and performance of state-owned enterprises (SOEs). The board has the ultimate responsibility, including through its fiduciary duty, for approving corporate strategies and overseeing SOE performance. In this capacity, the board may in effect act as an intermediary between the state as a shareholder and the company's executive management. According to the *OECD Guidelines on Corporate Governance of State-Owned Enterprises*, the board should act in the interest of both the state (and any other shareholders, where applicable) and the company.

The work of the board is becoming increasingly complex and demanding. Consistent with the *Guidelines*, in many countries the role of the board has been gradually altered from exercising a "compliance" function toward fulfilling a key role in setting and monitoring corporate strategies. Boards are more directly involved in corporate decision-making, which means that both the potential benefits and the downside risks of board work have grown in importance. In light of this, the state expects more of the boards than previously, especially with regard to their time commitment. The amount of time spent on board work has increased in recent years, and will probably continue to do so going forward.

For this reason, it is crucial that SOE board remuneration policies be designed with a view to attracting competent professionals and incentivising them to act in the best interest of each company and its shareholders.

Main findings

Actual remuneration levels

- While aggregate SOE board remuneration levels seem to stand significantly below those of private companies, on average, board members of commercially oriented SOEs receive higher fees than those of public policy-oriented SOEs, except in countries where remuneration is set by law. Variations also exist according to the size of SOEs and their sectors of operation.

- In almost all countries, the chair and vice chair of the board receive a higher remuneration than ordinary board members, which is most often equal to twice the allowance granted to other board members for the chair, and 1.25 to 1.5 times the regular amount for the vice chair. While board members may receive special compensation for their committee membership, as a general rule this is not very common, and is often decided for special cases or on an individual basis.

- Overall, while several countries report that low remuneration levels have hampered the recruitment of competent board members, some countries also mention the vocational element of service to the public interest as a key lever for competent professionals to consider board positions of SOEs, as it may be associated with prestige. Likewise, some countries also report that a board position in a SOE can be used as a stepping stone to better paid positions in the private sector. In such cases, robust conflict of interest provisions need to be implemented.

Remuneration policies and practices

- While board remuneration levels are formally approved by the AGM in almost all countries, different procedures exist across countries for setting the amounts of board fees. In countries with mainly commercial SOEs, remuneration seems to either be proposed by SOEs' remuneration committee or set by the central ownership unit based on private sector benchmarks. By contrast, in countries with policy-oriented SOEs – including those operating under monopoly situations, or with a majority of SOEs of "strategic interest", remuneration tends to either be set by law or based on public sector wage grids. Such measures have also been introduced in countries severely impacted by the 2008 global financial crisis, and have remained in place for the past decade. Some countries also report different procedures according to SOEs' corporate form, share of state ownership and listing status.

- Various policy approaches underpinning board remuneration exist across countries. In some countries, guidelines or principles on remuneration are set out in the state ownership policy, and are more or less detailed. In some countries, provisions are set by law. In other countries, no overarching policy/guidelines exist, but the law sets caps on remuneration. Overall, several factors need to be accounted for when devising a policy approach, including the prevailing laws and regulations, industry practices, size and complexity of the company, and their sector of operation.

- Caps on board remuneration are established by the state in three-quarters of the surveyed countries, and take various forms. They can be set at a percentage of the average annual remuneration of executive managers, based on the minimum monthly wages in the country, as a multiple of the lowest basic monthly salaries of the public sector wage grid, or at the absolute level. In countries where no government-wide caps exist, limits are usually established on an ad-hoc basis by the ownership entity. In some countries, a lower remuneration limit is also established.

Remuneration components

- There is considerable variation in the basis on which non-executive directors (including the members of supervisory boards) of SOEs across countries are remunerated. Non-executive directors can receive fixed fees, board meeting allowances, or a combination of both. Allowances to cover actual costs related to the board duties, including travelling, are in some cases added.

- Other forms of remuneration such as short-term bonuses and performance-related compensation are generally not granted to supervisory board members. In cases where bonuses are granted, consideration should be given to the fact that they may closely align the interest of non-executive directors with those of executive managers, and as such may compromise the independence of directors by encouraging management to take excessive short-term risks. In addition, performance targets should be carefully designed so that they are not "gamed" to improve pay.

- Remunerated civil servants on boards can give rise to potential conflicts of interest, as it may incentivise them to take on more directorships and to seek board membership in companies with the highest remuneration practices. Overall, in many countries where civil servants are allowed to serve on boards and are compensated, provisions have been introduced to limit the number of board seats that they may fill, as well as to cap their remuneration and to treat them like other independent members with regard to their selection, responsibilities and liabilities.

Transparency and disclosure practices

- In all but three of the surveyed countries, SOEs are required to disclose information on the remuneration levels of board members to the general public, albeit with varying levels of granularity: around two-thirds of surveyed countries require SOEs to do so for individual members, while they are required do so for the board as a whole in ten countries.

- In most countries, SOEs mainly release this information in their annual reports, which are subsequently made publicly available on their websites. While in the majority of surveyed countries SOEs are required to "proactively" disclose this information, in some countries, SOEs that are subject to the transparency act disclose this information only upon request.

- On average, individual SOEs disclose board remuneration information of greater granularity than the state. In some countries, a central online portal aggregating all remuneration information by all SOEs in the state's portfolio has been set up either by central government, the ownership entity or the central ownership agency, making this information readily accessible. While in some countries, the state does not "proactively" publish information about board remuneration levels, it publishes a compliance report on the implementation of disclosure requirements by SOEs. Overall, the state publishes information on board remuneration in around two-thirds of surveyed countries.

2.2. Actual remuneration levels of supervisory board members according to SOE corporate characteristics

2.2.1. Actual remuneration of ordinary board members

Variations according to SOE orientation

Overall, board members of commercially oriented SOEs receive higher annual nominal fees (USD 17 356 on average, representing 64% of average annual national wages) than those of public policy-oriented SOEs (USD 8 974 on average, representing 42% of average annual national wages), with the exception of **Croatia**, **Ireland** and **Turkey**, where fees are set by law or government decision (Figure 2.1). While annual nominal earnings of board members are highest in **Latvia**, **Chile**, the **Netherlands**, and **France** (Figure 2.1), these amounts are relatively modest when captured as percentages of average annual national wages (Figure 2.2).

Latvia stands as an exception with relatively high average annual nominal earnings of board members (USD 34 760 for board members of commercially oriented SOEs on average, and USD 20 391 for those of policy-oriented SOEs), which remain high when captured as a percentage of average annual wages (116% and 68%, respectively). This is because Latvia underwent substantial reform in 2015 to restore supervisory boards in the largest SOEs, and increase remuneration caps in order to attract professionals from the private sector and to better align with market levels. This has resulted in increasing board remuneration levels by approximately three times from 2015 to 2016.

Figure 2.1. Average annual remuneration of ordinary board members of SOEs (in USD as of 2020)

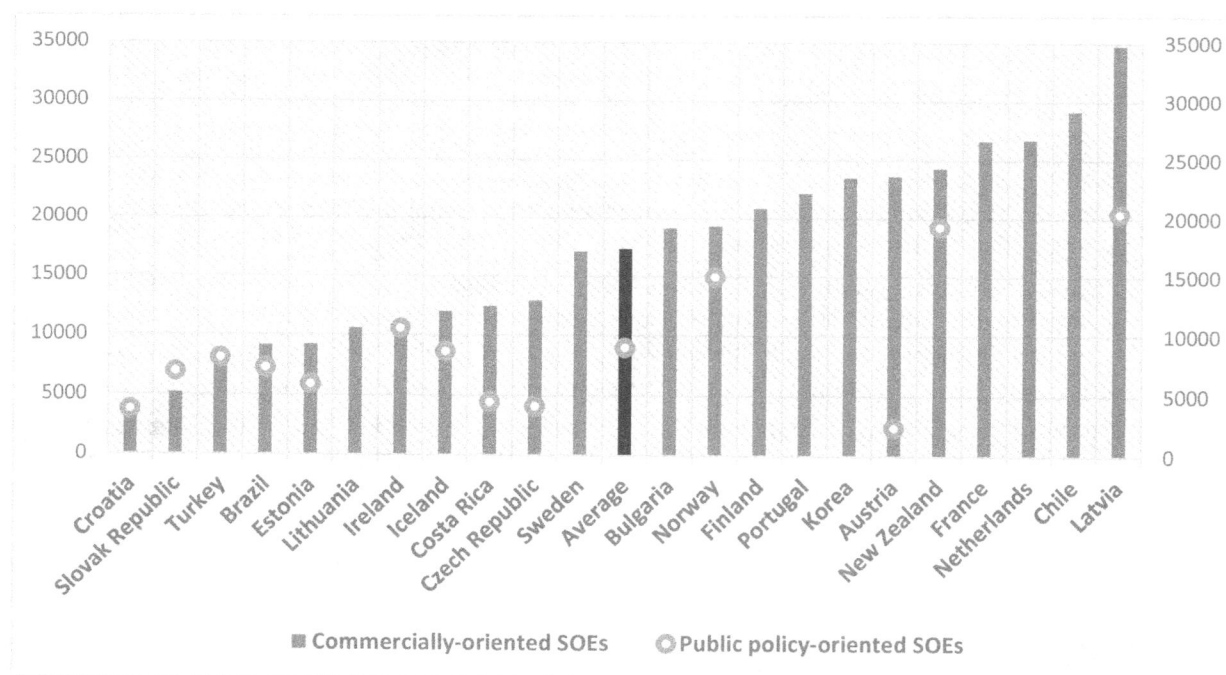

■ Commercially-oriented SOEs   ◎ Public policy-oriented SOEs

Note: Data covers SOEs with a state shareholding of at least 50% which are not listed on the stock exchange, except for **Chile**, where data includes one listed SOE (ZOFRI), albeit with remuneration levels similar to those of non-listed SOEs. For **Austria**, data for commercially oriented SOEs includes average remuneration amounts of board members of large SOEs only. In **Chile**, **France**, the **Netherlands**, **Portugal** and **Sweden**, all SOEs are classified as commercially oriented. Data for **Korea** includes amounts for public corporations only (hereby classified as "commercially oriented SOEs"), as data for quasi-governmental institutions is unavailable (hereby classified as "public policy-oriented SOEs"). For **Finland** and **Lithuania**, data includes all SOEs regardless of their orientation. For **Bulgaria**, data includes policy-oriented SOEs only.

Source: Author, based on country responses to the OECD questionnaire. For details, see Annex B.

In **Brazil**, **Costa Rica** and **Turkey**, high board wages displayed as a percentage of average annual national wages can likely be explained by low average nominal wages in these countries, and the need to set remuneration levels at a high threshold in order for them to remain competitive with private sector peers.

Figure 2.2. Average annual remuneration of ordinary board members of SOEs as a percentage of average annual national wages (as of 2020)

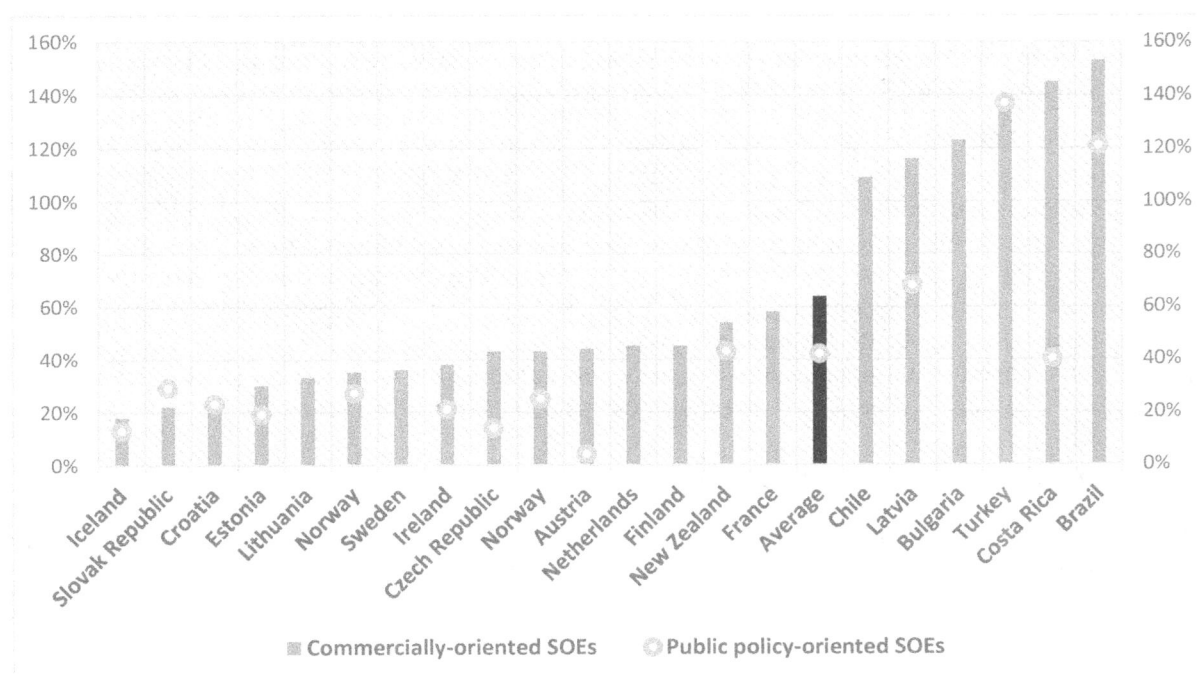

Note: Data covers SOEs with a state shareholding of at least 50%, which are not listed on the stock exchange, except for **Chile**, where data includes one listed SOE (ZOFRI), albeit with remuneration levels similar to those of non-listed SOEs. For **Austria**, data for commercially oriented SOEs includes average remuneration amounts of board members of large SOEs only. In **Chile**, **France**, the **Netherlands**, **Portugal** and **Sweden**, all SOEs are classified as commercially oriented. Data for **Korea** includes amounts for public corporations only (hereby classified as "commercially oriented SOEs"), as data for quasi-governmental institutions is unavailable (hereby classified as "public policy-oriented SOEs"). For **Finland** and **Lithuania**, data includes all SOEs regardless of their orientation. For **Bulgaria**, data includes policy-oriented SOEs only.
Source: Author, based on country responses to the OECD questionnaire, and calculations using the OECD database (https://data.oecd.org/earnwage/average-wages.htm) and ILOSTAT database (https://ilostat.ilo.org/topics/wages/). For details, see Annex B.

Variations according to SOE size and sector of operation

While many countries report that the remuneration of board members can vary considerably depending on the company size rather than on its sector of operation (e.g. **Lithuania**, **New Zealand**, **Sweden**), some countries report outliers in specific sectors. For instance, in the **Netherlands**, the average amounts of annual remuneration are significantly higher in the air transport sector, while they are slightly lower in this sector in **Croatia** (ranging from HRK 1 000 to 2000 of monthly remuneration).

Comparison with private sector levels

Regarding how board remuneration levels of SOEs fare against those of private peer companies, many countries report that they stand significantly below market levels. For instance, in **Greece**, for SOEs in the

HCAP's portfolio, board meeting allowances of listed companies amount to EUR 600, compared to EUR 240 for unlisted SOEs.[1] Likewise, in **Costa Rica**, evidence suggests[2] that board remuneration in SOEs generally sits below the levels of comparable private sector companies (Afanador, Bernal and Oneto, 2017[1]). In the **United Kingdom**, recent analysis also found that the highest UKGI non-executive director remuneration was GBP 40k, when the lowest of the FTSE 250 was GBP 51k. In **Ireland**, informal feedback from processes undertaken in making appointments to SOE boards suggests that remuneration levels in SOEs are substantially lower relative to comparable board roles in private sector companies.

In the **Netherlands**, a 2019 study found that while the average total remuneration of supervisory board members of listed index funds has increased by 187% over the past 15 years, which can be partly explained by an increase in the base fee and attendance fees, median total remuneration of supervisory board members of SOEs has increased by 18% since 2009, which is mainly explained by some indexation and in a number of cases by an increase in commission fees (Focus Orange, 2019[2]).

On the other hand, board remuneration seems to be on par with market levels in countries where remuneration is set based on private sector benchmarks, and sometimes by an external consultant, with a view of setting competitive – but not market-leading – fees. Overall, while several countries report that low remuneration levels have hampered the recruitment of competent board members, some countries also mention the vocational element of service to the public interest as a key lever for competent professionals to consider board positions of SOEs, as it may be associated with prestige (e.g. **Brazil**, **France**, **Spain**, **Turkey**, **United Kingdom**). Likewise, some countries also report that a board position in an SOE can be used as a stepping stone to better paid positions in the private sector (e.g. **New Zealand**). In such cases, robust conflict of interest provisions need to be implemented.

2.2.2. Actual remuneration of board chairs and vice chairs

The chair of the board carries a particular responsibility for organising the work of the board, for maintaining a dialogue with the management and the shareholders, and for devoting time to external representation of the company and other hospitality activities if relevant. As such, the chair of the board's remuneration should reflect the scope of the duties that the position entails.

In most countries, the chair and vice chair of the board receive a higher remuneration than ordinary board members, with the exception of **Brazil**, where undifferentiated amounts are granted to the board chair, vice chair and ordinary board members, as they are harmonised for all board members of commercially oriented SOEs (USD 9 148 on average) and public policy-oriented SOEs (USD 7 261 on average). Likewise, in **Croatia**, a fixed compensation rate for all board members regardless of their position on the board is set by law.

In many countries, the chair receives twice the allowance granted to other board members (e.g. **Chile**,[3] **Estonia**,[4] **New Zealand**, **Turkey**), and the vice chair receives 1.5 times (**Chile**) or 1.25 times (**New Zealand**) the amount paid to ordinary board members (Figure 2.3).

Figure 2.3. Comparing remuneration levels of board chairs and ordinary board members of commercially oriented and public policy-oriented SOEs

Shown as a percentage of average annual national wages

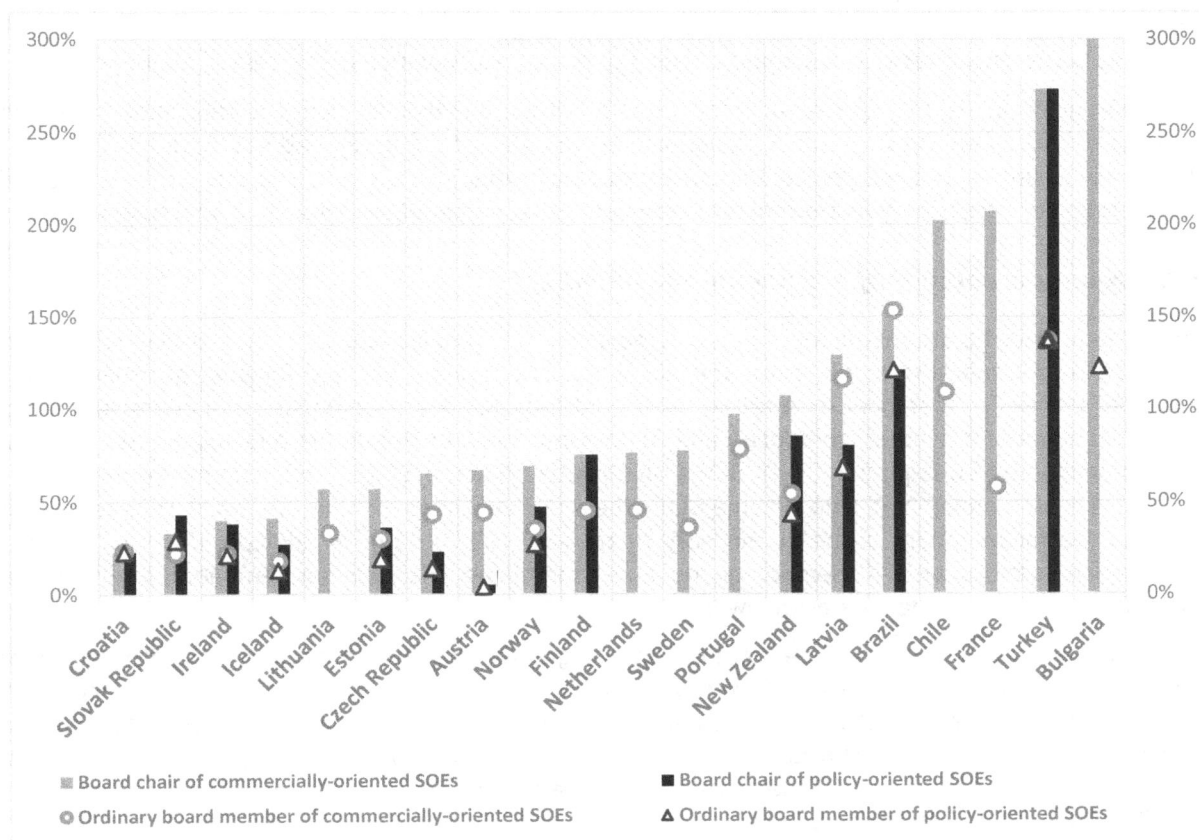

Note: Data includes non-listed SOEs with a state shareholding of at least 50%. In **France**, the **Netherlands** and **Portugal**, all SOEs are considered as commercially oriented. For **Finland** and **Lithuania**, data includes all SOEs irrespective of orientation. For **Austria**, data for commercially oriented SOEs includes average remuneration amounts of board members of large SOEs only.
Source: Author, based on country responses to the OECD questionnaire, and OECD calculations based on OECD database (https://data.oecd.org/earnwage/average-wages.htm) and ILOSTAT database (https://ilostat.ilo.org/topics/wages/). For details, see Annex B.

In some countries, the additional compensation granted to board chairs is lower. In the **Philippines**, the board chair is allowed an additional 20% of the standard rates for board meetings only, granted that he/she qualifies for the requirements of eligibility to compensation. In **Lithuania**, depending on the remuneration model adopted, the chair of the board may receive higher board meeting attendance allowances, or may be allowed to declare a higher number of hours spent for board member duties. In case the fixed annual remuneration model is used, the remuneration level is equivalent to 1.3 or 1.5 times the remuneration of ordinary board members. However, it is worth noting that according to Lithuanian law, the chair of the board has almost identical rights and duties as other board members, and thus his/her remuneration does not differ significantly from the amount paid to other board members.

Beyond this general rule of higher remuneration for the board chair and vice chair, special treatments also exist in some countries. For instance, in **Israel**, an active board chair (full-time) is entitled to the same remuneration as the CEO. In other cases (not an active chair), the chair is entitled to request an annual fixed pay, as opposed to board meeting allowances.

In **Costa Rica**, there is a considerable difference between chairpersonship of the board in SOEs that have the "Executive President" figure,[5] and those that have a non-executive chair. The Executive President is responsible for chairing the board, for overseeing the CEO, and is also involved to varying degrees in the administrative aspects of the company. As such, the Executive President position receives a fixed monthly remuneration, which is not homogenous across SOEs, and can be between two to six times higher than the monthly meeting attendance allowance that would be granted to a non-executive chair. Of note, non-executive board chairs receive the same meeting attendance allowance as the rest of the board.

In **Latvia**, since 2016, the remuneration of the chair of the supervisory board is calculated by applying respective coefficients (from 1.5 to 3, depending on the size of the enterprise set by regulations) to the statistically determined average monthly salary of employees in the country in the previous year. The remuneration of supervisory board ordinary members is capped at 90% of the chair's remuneration.

2.2.3. Remuneration of board committee members

Board members who are members of board committees may receive special compensation for this work. However, as a general rule this is not very common, and is often decided for special cases or on an individual basis. For instance, in **Austria**, additional fees for board committee memberships are only granted in some of the larger, competing and listed companies. In **Brazil**, the audit committee is the only paid committee which is present in all SOEs. In **Croatia**, in some SOEs, audit committee members are usually paid per meeting held, and in some SOEs they receive a fixed monthly fee, which is generally lower than the fee for members of the supervisory board (e.g. HRK 1 500). In addition, if a member of the supervisory board is also a member of the audit committee, then his/her remuneration in the audit committee is in some instances even lower.

When additional fees for committee membership are granted, they are often capped (**Estonia**, **Greece**, **Latvia**, **Lithuania**, **Peru**, **Portugal**) (Box 2.1). For instance, In **Latvia**, while there can be additional fees for committee membership, the overall remuneration cannot exceed the cap set in *Cabinet Regulations*. Likewise, in **Portugal**, according to Article 29 of Decree-Law No. 71/2007 of 27 March, fees granted to non-executive board members for their participation in a committee are set by government according to a classification of SOEs into three groups.

Box 2.1. Provisions on remuneration granted for board committee membership: examples from selected countries

In **Estonia**, while the remuneration of committee members is decided by the shareholder, some restrictions apply: i) committee members get paid only for the month when there was a committee meeting; ii) the monthly remuneration of a committee member can be up to 25% of the remuneration of a supervisory board member; iii) the aggregate fee for participating in the committees can be up to 50% of the remuneration of a board member; and iv) the chair of a committee can receive an additional 25% compared to ordinary members.

In **Lithuania**, board members are compensated for their membership in board committees (if such committees are established). Typically, a similar compensation model is used for both work at board level and at board committees. However, actual remuneration levels are lower than those granted for board membership. For example, the hourly rate ranges from EUR 30 to EUR 75 and in most cases cannot exceed 1/15 of the annual CEO salary. Based on data from 2020, committee members' remuneration accounted for around 30-35% of board members' annual remuneration, while it accounted for 45% of the remuneration of the chair of the committee. Overall, there is no unified regulation regarding remuneration of the committees and actual remuneration levels are set by shareholding entities and boards themselves.

In **Peru**, directors may receive additional compensation for their participation in board committees, with the following conditions: i) the compensation amount for board committee participation is equivalent to 50% of the remuneration that is granted to the directors for their participation on a board; ii) in the case of the chairpersons that receive monthly fixed compensation and attendance allowances per meeting, they cannot receive additional compensation for committee membership; iii) the directors can receive a maximum of one retribution per month for participating in one or more committees; iv) civil servants receive a payment for their participation in any board committee.

In **Greece**, committee members and chairs of listed SOEs receive an annual fixed compensation and attendance allowances (EUR 13 000 fixed fee for the board committee chair or EUR 11 000 fixed fee for committee members, plus EUR 400 per meeting), while committee members of non-listed SOEs receive in principle only attendance allowances (EUR 50 per committee meeting).

Source: Author, based on questionnaire responses.

In **Sweden**, for fees to be paid for service on a committee, the work involved has to be of a substantial extent. Likewise, in **New Zealand**, a case has been made for special fees to be granted to the chair of an audit and risk committee in case of particularly high workload, however, this is more of an exception. Under the *Cabinet Fees Framework*, chairs of committees can get a 10% loading if they are not simultaneously acting as board chairs or vice chairs. In the **United Kingdom**, while the vast majority of boards do not pay additional fees for chairing or sitting on a board committee, there are some instances where committee chairs may receive additional allowances, ranging from GBP 5k-10k per annum. Likewise, in **Iceland**, very few SOEs may grant additional fees for board committee membership, and include mainly the banks.

Overall, in the majority of surveyed countries, board members do not usually receive additional fees for committee membership (**Chile**, **Colombia**, **Costa Rica**, **Ireland**, **Korea**, **Mexico**, **Turkey**),[6] or are only additionally compensated in special cases (**Iceland**, **New Zealand**, **Sweden**, **United Kingdom**).

2.3. Remuneration policies and practices

The *SOE Guidelines* state that the remuneration of both SOE boards and executive management should be aligned with the long-term interest of the enterprise. With regard to the boards of directors, they further posit that "[t]here is a strong case for aligning the remuneration of board members of SOEs with private sector practices" (annotations to Chapter II point F).

Overall, board remuneration practices and levels seem to depend to a certain extent on countries' ownership arrangements and their SOEs' corporate characteristics. This section considers remuneration policies and practices applicable to supervisory board members (or non-executive directors) of unlisted and majority-owned SOEs, including the procedures in place for deciding remuneration amounts of board members, their remuneration components, as well as provisions regarding board composition (i.e. whether civil servants are allowed to serve on boards and are compensated).

2.3.1. Remuneration models

While board remuneration levels are formally approved by the AGM in almost all countries, different procedures exist across countries for setting the amounts of board fees. Evidence suggests that board remuneration policies and practices differ according to countries' ownership model, the degree of corporatisation of SOEs, and board composition (i.e. majority of independent members or civil servants).[7] In particular, in countries with mainly commercial SOEs, remuneration seems to either be proposed by SOEs' remuneration committee or set by the central ownership unit based on private sector benchmarks. By contrast, in countries with policy-oriented SOEs – including those operating under monopoly situations, or with a majority of SOEs of "strategic interest", remuneration tends to either be set by law or based on public sector wage grids. Such measures have also been introduced in countries severely impacted by the 2008 global financial crisis, and have remained in place for the past decade (Figure 2.4). Some countries also report different procedures according to SOEs' corporate form, share of state ownership and listing status. Detailed information on individual countries' approaches is provided in Table 2.4.

Figure 2.4. How is board remuneration decided?

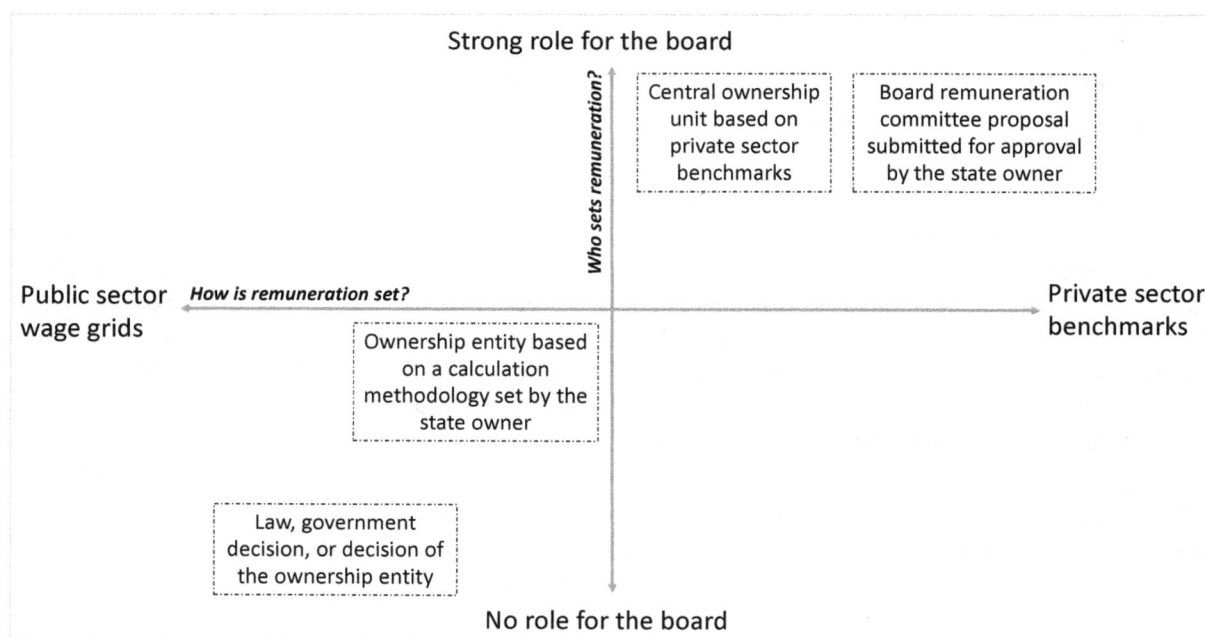

Source: Author's own elaboration.

Remuneration is proposed by the remuneration committee for approval by the general shareholders' meeting

In **Belgium**, **Brazil**, **France**, **Iceland**, **Japan**, **Korea**, the **Netherlands** and the **United Kingdom**, the board remuneration committee of individual SOEs formulates a board remuneration proposal, which is submitted for approval by the general shareholders' meeting. Although this practice seems to be in place in countries with a mix of ownership models, this process – which is akin to private company practice – seems to be better suited for commercially oriented SOEs operating in competitive markets in order to attract competent professionals. While in **Belgium**, the role of the remuneration committee is provided by law, in **France** and **Korea**, after remuneration limits have been approved at the AGM, the board has full discretion on how to allocate this pool of fees among board members. In the **Netherlands**, the Ministry of Finance and the board usually try to find an agreement on the board proposal during informal meetings, before formalising the policy during the AGM. In the **United Kingdom**, while remuneration committees are generally responsible for benchmarking and establishing remuneration policies which are submitted to line ministries for approval, in certain cases secondary approval from the Chief Secretary to the Treasury may be required.

Remuneration is set by the central ownership unit based on private sector benchmarks

In **Austria**, **Finland**, **Norway** and **Sweden**, where ownership is centralised, board remuneration is set based on private sector benchmarks, and sometimes by an external consultant, with a view of setting competitive – but not market-leading – fees. For instance, in **Sweden**, ahead of the general meeting's decision on directors' fees, the Government Office carries out an analysis comparing fee levels with the fees paid by comparable companies (~300 listed companies, Nasdaq OMX). In **Norway**, the state carries out a specific assessment of each company's remuneration of governing bodies before the general meeting, and comparable Norwegian companies will normally be used as a frame of reference when stipulating the remuneration. Overall, these countries report that board remuneration is usually on par with market levels.

Box 2.2. Norway's remuneration policy

According to the Report to the Storting on State Ownership:

- Remuneration should reflect the board's responsibility, expertise, time commitment and the complexity of the company's activities, in accordance with the *Norwegian Code of Practice for Corporate Governance*. Comparable Norwegian companies will normally be used as a frame of reference when stipulating the remuneration.

- Remuneration should be at a moderate level. This means that the remuneration shall not be higher than what is necessary to ensure relevant expertise on the board, and should reflect the board's responsibilities and workload.

In practice, the Norwegian state carries out a specific assessment of each company's remuneration of governing bodies before the general meeting. The state will normally propose, or, in companies with a nomination committee, endorse growth in line with the general wage growth in Norway in cases where the state considers the board's remuneration to be at the correct level. This is both to ensure moderation and to maintain an appropriate level over time.

Of note, the state will only propose or endorse a bigger increase in remuneration if the level is considered to be too low to achieve the best possible composition of the board and seen in relation to an assessment of the board's responsibility, expertise, time commitment and the complexity of the company's activities. This means that an increase in remuneration that significantly exceeds general wage growth is only acceptable when it is necessary to contribute to ensuring that the remuneration is at the right level, especially to be able to attract the necessary expertise.

The state will propose or endorse zero growth if the level of remuneration is deemed to be too high. There may also be cases where there are grounds for reducing the remuneration, for example if the company's scope of activities or complexity is materially reduced.

Overall, Norwegian companies will normally be used as the frame of reference in this assessment. Since 2010, the Norwegian Institute of Directors has conducted board remuneration surveys of companies listed on the Oslo Stock Exchange and companies with a state ownership interest. The 2018 survey shows that Equinor, Telenor, Yara International and Norsk Hydro, which are partly owned by the state and are among the biggest companies on the Oslo Stock Exchange in terms of market value, are not among the companies that pay the highest remuneration to the chair or members of the board.

Source: Norwegian Government (2019), *Report to the Sorting*, https://www.regjeringen.no/en/dokumenter/meld.-st.-8-20192020/id2678758/

Remuneration is set by the ownership entity based on a calculation methodology set by government

In **Bulgaria**, the **Czech Republic**, **Estonia** and **New Zealand**, where ownership tends to be decentralised (except for New Zealand), remuneration tends to be decided by the ownership entity following a calculation methodology set by the government owner, which may differ according to SOEs' orientation and sector of operation. For instance, in **Bulgaria**, board and executive remuneration is calculated by the application of a total score determined by several variables, using key performance indicators (KPIs) provided by law (Annex 2 of the Implementing Rules of the Law in Public Enterprises). However, shareholding ministries have ultimate discretion on the policies, rules and guidelines of the remuneration of board members and executive managers of SOEs in their respective portfolio, and can thus decide to reduce remuneration levels by changing the value of the score unit. The terms of remuneration are included in management contracts of board and executive managers, and the calculations themselves are carried out by individual SOEs.

In **New Zealand**, different methodologies exist for SOEs depending on their orientation. For *Crown company boards*, the Treasury advises the shareholding ministers on appropriate fees according to the Crown Company Fees Methodology, which evaluates companies under nine factors and then allocates a benchmarked points ranking. The Treasury then provides these rankings to an independent remuneration specialist, who provides comparative private sector rates. For *non-company Crown entities*, the Treasury advises the shareholding minister on remuneration in accordance with the Cabinet Fees Framework. Overall, the shareholding ministers annually approve a fees' pool for each board, which then determines how to allocate this pool of fees. While the base rate used to calculate the fees' pool for directorships ranges from USD 18 000 to USD 54 500 per annum per director, the actual rate depends on a number of factors, including the size and complexity of the company and the diversity of its operations and markets, and associated risk profile.

Remuneration is fixed and is set by law, by government decision or by a decision of the ownership entity

In **Australia**, **Colombia**, **Costa Rica**, **Croatia**, **Ireland**, **Israel**, **Mexico**, **Peru**, **Philippines**, **Portugal** and **Turkey**, where mixed ownership models exist, remuneration is usually fixed and set by law, by government decision, or by a decision of the ownership entity. It may be inferred that this model is used in countries where SOEs are mainly tasked with the delivery of public services and/or operate under monopoly situations, and as such may be viewed as an extension of the public sector (whereby public sector wage grids are to be used to determine the amounts of board remuneration). This model may also be in place in countries with a majority of SOEs of "strategic interest", where board autonomy is limited. In countries severely impacted by the 2008 global financial crisis (e.g. **Croatia**, **Portugal**), board remuneration levels are set by law and have not evolved for the past decade. This is also the case for the **Philippines**, where the per diems, allowances, incentives, and compensation structure for the members of supervisory boards have been set out by the central ownership agency in 2011 according to five categories of SOEs (Annex A). These levels have been maintained since 2011.

While some countries may seek to determine a remuneration reference rate for directors that is commensurate with their roles and responsibilities and may also consider directors' workload, private sector fees, and wage indices (e.g. **Australia**), some countries where remuneration is set by law report that as levels have remained static for the past decade (and are not indexed on inflation), this does not allow to attract competent professionals (e.g. **Croatia**, the **Philippines**).

Box 2.3. SOE board remuneration in Costa Rica

In **Costa Rica**, remuneration policies are established in the legal framework of SOEs, either in their statutory laws or articles of incorporation. Overall, five different calculation methods exist:

- *Method 1*: the board meeting attendance allowance is established by the Council of Ministers.
- *Method 2*: the way to calculate the board meeting attendance allowance is set in the SOE statutory law.
- *Method 3*: the board meeting attendance allowance is established as 10% of the base salary of the Comptroller General (the chief of the supreme audit institution).
- *Method 4*: the board meeting attendance allowance is established as 10% of the fixed component of a congressperson's monthly remuneration[8].
- *Method 5*: the board meeting attendance allowance is established by *Law N. 7 138 "Extraordinary budget law" of 16 November 1989*, which set the initial value at USD 4.8 and its automatic yearly adjustment according to the Consumer Price Index.

Of note, the methods are not mutually exclusive, and sometimes do overlap for some SOEs. For example, for the two state-owned banks and the insurance company, the statutory laws point to the Council of Ministers to set the remuneration (Method 1), and this Council chose to establish their remuneration as 10% of the base salary of the Comptroller General (Method 3).

Table 2.1. Application of the five calculation methods to each SOE in Costa Rica

Method	Description	SOE applicable
1	The board meeting attendance allowance is established by the Council of Ministers	INS, BCR, BNCR
2	The way to calculate the board meeting attendance allowance is set in the SOE statutory law	INCOFER
3	The board meeting attendance allowance is established as 10% of the base salary of the Comptroller General (the chief of the supreme audit institution)	Costa Rica Mail Service, ICE
4	The board meeting attendance allowance is established as 10% of the fixed component of a congressperson's monthly remuneration	SINART
5	The board meeting attendance allowance is established by Law N. 7 138 "Extraordinary budget law" of 16 November 1989, which set the initial value at USD 4.8 and its automatic yearly adjustment according to the Consumer Price Index	RECOPE, FANAL, JAPDEVA, AYA, INCOP, JPS

Note: General guidelines include Law N. 3065, Article 2, Law N. 7138, Article 60, and Law N. 9635, articles 43, 44. The remuneration policies are set in the following legal frameworks: INCOFER (Law 7001, Article 10), INS (Law 12, Article 5), JPS (Law 8718, Article 3), BCR (Law 1644, Article 33), BNCR (Law 1644, Article 33), ICE (Law 449, Article 10), INCOP (Law 1721, Article 10), AyA (Law 2726, Article 10), JAPDEVA (Law 3091, Article 14), FANAL (Law 2035, Article 24), Correos de Costa Rica (Law 7768, articles 7, 15).
Source: Country response to the OECD questionnaire.

2.3.2. Remuneration policies

Various policy approaches underpinning board remuneration exist across countries. In some countries, guidelines or principles on remuneration are set out in the state ownership policy, and are more or less detailed. In some countries, provisions are set by law. For instance, in **Belgium** the law provides for the formal role of the remuneration committee, while in **Bulgaria** the law sets KPIs to be negotiated between the ownership entity and the SOE. In some countries, there are no overarching policy/guidelines, but the law sets caps on remuneration. Overall, several factors need to be accounted for when devising a policy approach, including the prevailing laws and regulations, industry practices, size and complexity of the company, and their sector of operation.

Table 2.2. Types of board remuneration policies

Type of remuneration policies	Country
Guidelines/principles on remuneration within the State Ownership Policy or otherwise	Austria, the Czech Republic, Germany, Hungary, Iceland, Ireland, Korea, Latvia, the Netherlands, New Zealand, Norway, Sweden
Provisions set by law, including statutory laws and SOEs' articles of association	Australia, Belgium, Bulgaria, Costa Rica, Estonia, Croatia, Lithuania, Mexico, Peru, Philippines, Portugal, the Slovak Republic, Turkey,
No remuneration policy/guidelines, but law sets caps	Brazil, Colombia, France, Greece, Spain, United Kingdom

Source: Author, based on an analysis of questionnaire responses.

Caps on remuneration

While caps on board remuneration exist in a large majority of surveyed countries (27 out of 36), they take various forms. They can be set at a percentage of the average annual remuneration of executive managers (e.g. **Austria**, **Brazil**, **Lithuania**, **Portugal**), based on the minimum or average monthly wages in the country (e.g. **Bulgaria, Colombia, Latvia**), as a multiple of the lowest basic monthly salaries of the public sector wage grid (e.g. **Costa Rica**), or at the absolute level (e.g. **France, Korea**). In countries where no cross-government caps exist, limits are usually established on an ad-hoc basis (based on a private sector benchmarking) by the ownership entity (e.g. **Finland**) or by the Prime Minister's Office (e.g. **Sweden**). In some countries, a lower limit on remuneration is also established (e.g. **Austria**).

2.3.3. Remuneration components

There is considerable variation in the basis on which non-executive directors (including the members of supervisory boards) of SOEs across countries are remunerated, as well as the sums they receive. Non-executive directors can receive fixed fees, board meeting allowances, or a combination of both. Allowances to cover actual costs related to the board duties, including travelling, are in some cases added.

Overall, other forms of remuneration such as short-term bonuses and performance-related compensation are generally not granted to supervisory board members. In cases where bonuses are granted, consideration should be given to the fact that they may closely align the interest of non-executive directors with those of executive managers, and as such may compromise the independence of directors by encouraging management to take excessive short-term risks. In addition, attention should be paid to carefully design performance targets so that they are not "gamed" to improve pay. Overall, while variable remuneration components can help attract and motivate directors, careful consideration should be given to the amount of a director's pay that should be linked to performance targets.

Figure 2.5. Remuneration components

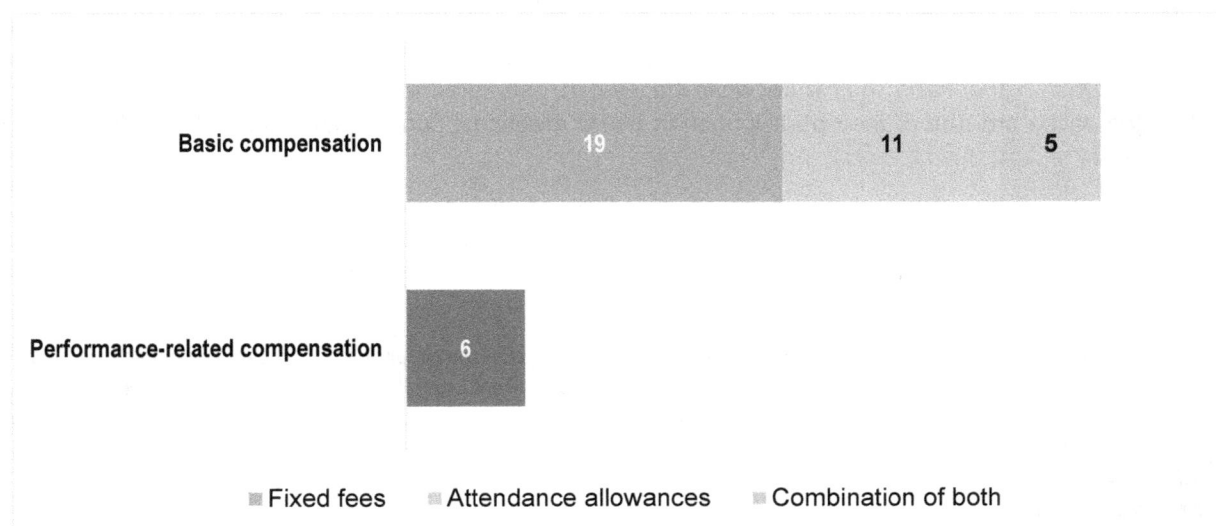

Note: Data for basic components (including the "fixed fees", "attendance allowances" and "both" categories) is based out of a total of 35 countries, as Lithuania stands in a category of its own (see Box 2.4). Data on variable components is based out of a total of 36 countries.
Source: Author, based on questionnaire responses and desk research. See Table 2.4 for details.

Basic component

Fixed fees

The majority of surveyed countries (54%) set fixed fees or pay for board members, where remuneration is not linked to board meeting attendance. However, some of the countries that follow this model also allow board meeting allowances to be granted on an ad-hoc basis. For instance, in **Iceland**, while most companies compensate board members on a monthly basis, some smaller companies only compensate board members for attending meetings as they have fewer meetings during the year.

In some countries, board members are also entitled to the reimbursement of their travel expenses in addition to their fixed compensation (**Croatia**, **Hungary**, **Norway**, **United Kingdom**). Some countries also grant special allowances in addition to the basic compensation paid to directors for attending their duties, including attending board and committee meetings, meeting preparation, stakeholder management, and any other agreed tasks. For instance, in **New Zealand**, crown companies may request approval for additional special purpose fees in response to an identified business need, and each request is considered by the responsible Ministers on its merits. Fees may also be granted for the professional development of directors, with a guiding rate of between NZD 2 000- 4 000 per director, and up to NZD 10 000 for attending courses at the Institute of Directors. There is no limit for these fees, as they are granted on a case-by-case basis. In only a few countries, remuneration is calculated based on the amount of the annual minimum wage (**Hungary**), or based on the average monthly or nominal wage (**Latvia** and the **Slovak Republic**, respectively).

Board meeting allowances

Eleven of the 36 surveyed countries compensate board members with board meeting attendance allowances only, which are usually calculated on the basis of the number of attended meetings. However, in some countries, some restrictions apply. For instance, in **Chile**, board members are paid for a limited number of sessions per month. Likewise, in **Peru**, directors are paid for only two meetings per month.

In **Colombia** and the **Philippines**, the maximum amount of allowances that board members can receive per meeting and per year is based on the national classification scheme, which takes into account their total amounts of assets (Table 2.3). Likewise, in **Costa Rica**, the methodology for calculating the amount of allowances that can be granted is set in the companies' statutory laws or articles of incorporation (Box 2.3). On the other hand, in **France**, while the level of remuneration of board members is systematically calculated at the pro-rata of their participation in board meetings, compensation can also include a fixed component.

Table 2.3. Criteria for setting board remuneration in Colombian SOEs

In Colombian Pesos (COP)

Levels of SOE assets	Maximum board meeting allowances for board and board committee members (as a multiple of Current Legal Monthly Minimum Wages SMMLV)
Greater than COP 15 Bn	6
COP 5 to COP 15 Bn	4,5
COP 2.5 to COP 5 Bn	4
COP 1 to COP 2.5 Bn	3
COP 500.000 to COP 1 Bn	2,75
COP 250.000 to COP 500.000	2,5
COP 100.000 to COP 250.000	2
Less than COP 100.000	1,5

Note: As of September 2021, the Current Legal Monthly Minimum Wage (SMMLV) is COP 908.526.
Source: Country response to the OECD questionnaire.

In some countries, board members are also eligible for the reimbursement of travel expenses (**Colombia, Estonia, Finland, Germany, Peru**). In **Finland**, in some companies, remuneration may be lifted by up to 50% for board members who live abroad. In **Colombia**, in order to incentivise the use of technology for remotely based board members, a recent decree (Decree 767 of 2020) allows board members attending meetings virtually to receive the same remuneration as those attending meetings physically, which was not previously the case.

Combination of fixed pay and attendance allowances

In only a few countries (5 out of 36), fixed pay and attendance allowances are combined. In **Belgium** and **Mexico**, board remuneration comprises a fixed amount, as well as a variable component consisting of attendance fees. In **Korea**, non-executive directors usually receive a monthly allowance and a monthly attendance allowance, while some institutions only grant board meeting attendance allowance without an additional fixed monthly component. While board members with similar duties basically receive similar pay, remuneration levels may slightly differ according to seniority.

Box 2.4. Board remuneration models in Lithuania

Three compensation models currently exist in Lithuania. Remuneration is most often based on **hourly rates**, whereby board members are required to fill in activity reports in order to get their reported hours compensated. While this model is mandatory for statutory enterprises, some limited liability companies have adopted this model as well. The rate usually ranges from EUR 50 to EUR 100 per hour.

Another common practice is to link remuneration to **board meeting attendance**, whereby board members are compensated based on the number of board meetings attended.

In such cases, the rate usually ranges from EUR 100 to EUR 300 per board meeting. A system of **fixed annual remuneration** may be used as well.

It is worth noting that the state plans to unify board remuneration systems by abandoning the hourly remuneration model (due to extensive administrative burdens and various inefficiencies), and shifting to the fixed annual remuneration model.

Source: Author, based on questionnaire responses.

Variable component

In the vast majority of surveyed countries (83%), SOE board members do not receive any performance-related compensation. Indeed, bonuses as a share of profit can be granted to board members of specific SOEs in only six of the 36 surveyed countries (**Bulgaria**, **Chile**, the **Czech Republic**, **Peru**, **Philippines**, the **Slovak Republic**). Of note, although this is legally allowed in **Lithuania** and **Peru**, this is not actually practiced by SOEs, as no such cases have been recorded to date.

Box 2.5. Provisions underpinning performance-related compensation of supervisory board members in selected countries (Bulgaria, Chile, the Slovak Republic)

Bulgaria

The members of the executive and supervisory bodies of the enterprises shall receive bonuses beyond the amounts of remuneration if the accounting profit increases during the accounting year compared to the previous year and provided that the company does not have an uncovered loss from previous years and arrears. The money shall be charged to the profit after its taxation and the allocation of statutory portions thereof to the reserve of the company, deductions from profits or a dividend in favour of the owner of the capital at an amount determined by the general meeting of the shareholders, from one to three average monthly remuneration received during the current year by the members of the executive and supervisory bodies. No other benefits or remuneration are foreseen.

Chile

Performance-related compensation is granted to board members, except for some SOEs (EFE, Correos, ENAP, CODELCO, TVN, BCO Estado, ENAMI). In port companies, the variable income for meeting goals can double the allowance for attending sessions. In the case of listed and unlisted enterprises, the variable remuneration can reach approximately 40% of the remuneration for meeting attendance.

This variable component is based on agreed objectives between the ownership entity (Sistema de Empresas Públicas – SEP) and the companies' boards of directors, and are specified with indicators of strategic, financial, operational and corporate governance nature, among others.

Performance-related compensation is also capped, depending on the type of company and the position of the board member within the board of directors. The limits are annual and the maximum variable compensation for the year will be the product of a combination of parameters, including the percentage of compliance with the "Goal Agreement" (i.e. agreement on objectives), and the percentage of attendance of board meetings during the year.

Slovak Republic

A share on profit/royalties can be granted to supervisory board members of statutory SOEs (or "state enterprises" regulated by the *Act No. 111/1990 Coll. on State Enterprise*), and is calculated based on the amount granted to the CEO of the state enterprise.

In particular, while the monthly salary of the CEO of a state enterprise cannot exceed eight times the average wage of the previous year and the annual remuneration (share on profit/royalties) cannot exceed 10% of the disposal profit of the enterprise, the monthly salary of a supervisory board member cannot exceed five times the average wage of the previous year and the amount of the annual remuneration (share on profit/royalties) corresponds to 5% of the amount granted to the CEO of the state enterprise.

Source: Author, based on country responses to the OECD questionnaire, supplemented by desk research.

2.3.4. Provisions regarding civil servants and direct state representatives on boards

Remunerated civil servants on boards can give rise to potential conflicts of interest, as it may incentivise them to take on more directorships and to seek board membership in companies with the highest remuneration practices. As such, good practice calls for limiting the number of board seats that may be held by civil servants, as well as capping their remuneration. Overall, remunerated civil servants on boards should be treated like other independent members with regard to their selection, responsibilities and liabilities.

Civil servants/state officials can serve on boards under the same conditions as independent board members

In a third of surveyed countries, civil servants and other direct state representatives can serve on SOE boards under the same conditions as independent board members, including functions and remuneration (**Austria**, **Belgium**, **Bulgaria**, **Chile**, **Colombia**, the **Czech Republic**, **Finland**, **Hungary**, **Latvia**, **Peru**, **Portugal**). However, several of these countries have implemented limitations on the composition of boards, in particular regarding the number of board seats that may be filled by civil servants or state representatives, as well as on the number of boards that they are allowed to serve. Some of these countries have also implemented caps on the maximum compensation that civil servants or other state officials are allowed to receive (Box 2.6).

Box 2.6. Provisions regarding civil servants on boards: Selected country examples

Provisions regarding the maximum number of boards seats that may be filled by civil servants

In **Latvia**, civil servants or direct state representatives can serve on SOE boards, provided that the board be composed of a majority of independent members. In addition, civil servants should participate in the open nomination procedure as any other candidate, and receive the same remuneration as other board members for conducting the same functions. Likewise, in **Bulgaria**, according to the *Implementation Rules of the SOE Act*, civil servants and other state representatives can serve on boards, granted that boards be comprised of at least one-third and not more than half of independent board members. In **Colombia**, according to *Article 19 of Law 4 of 1992*, public officials can receive remuneration from up to two boards. In **Hungary**, *Act 122 of 2009 on the more efficient operation of*

SOEs provides that one person may be remunerated for a maximum of one management board member position and one supervisory board member position.

Caps on remuneration of civil servant board members

In the **Czech Republic**, the total sum of compensations paid to a civil servant for their membership in executive or supervisory bodies of SOEs for a calendar year should not exceed 25% of the annual amount of the highest state service pay tariff. In **Chile**, boards may include a maximum of two civil servants. In addition, senior state officials[9] who receive special allowances may not serve on more than one board, and their monthly remuneration may not exceed the equivalent of USD 1 676. Of note however, civil servants cannot sit on the board of SOEs under the oversight of SEP. In **Peru**, while civil servants can serve on several boards simultaneously, they can only be remunerated for their participation on one of them, with the exception of teachers at public universities who are entitled to receive additional remuneration, as provided by *Article 38 of Law no. 30 057 (Ley del Servicio Civil)*, and by FONAFE's *Guidelines for the Management of Directories and Directors*. Civil servants also cannot be remunerated for integrating board committees. In addition, while other state officials are allowed to serve on boards albeit unremunerated, no such cases have been recorded to date.

Source: Author, based on questionnaire responses.

Civil servants – but not other state officials – can serve on boards under the same conditions as independent board members

In another quarter of surveyed countries, civil servants – but not other state officials – are allowed to serve on SOE boards. In some cases, they are subject to the same remuneration conditions and limitations as other board members (**Brazil**, **Croatia, Estonia, Germany, Greece, Spain**). In **Croatia**, this is provided by the *Law on the Prevention of Conflicts of Interest*. In **Estonia**, Secretary Generals of ministries are also not allowed to serve on boards, as they are members of the Nomination Committee whose role is to propose candidates to SOE supervisory boards.

While civil servants are allowed to serve on SOE boards in **Costa Rica**, the **Philippines** and **Turkey**, their remuneration is conditional to certain provisions. In **Costa Rica**, civil servants may only receive attendance allowances if board meetings are not held during the working hours of their affiliated institution. In some cases, the statutory laws or articles of incorporation of certain SOEs designate civil servants on boards without voting rights. In the **Philippines,** public officials can be appointed to boards, and can only receive remuneration for their participation to board committee meetings (limited to the rates under EO No/ 24). They are also eligible to receive performance-based incentives. However, they are not eligible to receive any other form of compensation (such as salaries, allowances, benefits and bonuses). In **Turkey**, civil servants may serve on SOE boards and receive the same compensation as other members. However, if they become a member of the board of more than one corporation, they can only receive compensation from one corporation, in addition to their primary salaries as civil servants.

Civil servants/state officials can serve on boards and are uncompensated

On the other hand, in seven of the 36 surveyed countries, civil servants or other direct state representatives may be appointed to SOE boards subject to conflict of interest provisions, but do not receive compensation (**France**, **Israel**, **Lithuania**, **Mexico**, the **Slovak Republic**, **Sweden**, **United Kingdom**). In **France**, SOEs are legally required to include at least one civil servant or state representative on their boards. Civil servants serve on boards subject to conditions relative to cumulative employment and their remuneration is the same as for other board members, although it is systematically paid in full to the state. Likewise, in **Lithuania**, civil servants may serve on SOE boards and are required to conduct the same functions as other board members. While civil servants who serve on SOE boards are not compensated, statutory SOEs incur costs related to civil servants' performance as board members, but remuneration is transferred to the state budget. In the **United Kingdom**, civil servants or direct state representatives may serve on SOE boards, with special clauses inserted in their contracts to enable them to continue in both roles and deal with any potential conflicts. While they are not usually remunerated as per government's policy, they are however indemnified for legal protection. In the **Slovak Republic**, *Act No. 55/2017 Coll. on service in state administration* provides that civil servants or state representatives are not entitled to any remuneration when acting on the boards of commercially oriented SOEs. In **Sweden**, civil servants may be remunerated only in special cases following a decision by the general meeting, although in practice this usually never happens as investment directors who are board members are not remunerated, and other civil servants on boards are extremely rare.

Civil servants are appointed on boards only under exceptional circumstances, or are not allowed to serve on boards

In a minority of countries, civil servants may be appointed to SOE boards only in exceptional circumstances or for special reasons, such as major restructuring (**Australia, Iceland, Japan, New Zealand, Switzerland**). In **Japan,** when civil servants are appointed on boards, they generally have no voting rights. Overall, civil servants are not allowed to serve on SOE boards under any circumstances in only three of the surveyed countries (**Korea**, the **Netherlands, Norway**). In **Ireland**, as a general rule, neither civil servants nor other state officials serve on the boards of commercial state entities.

Figure 2.6. Can civil servants or other state officials serve on boards?

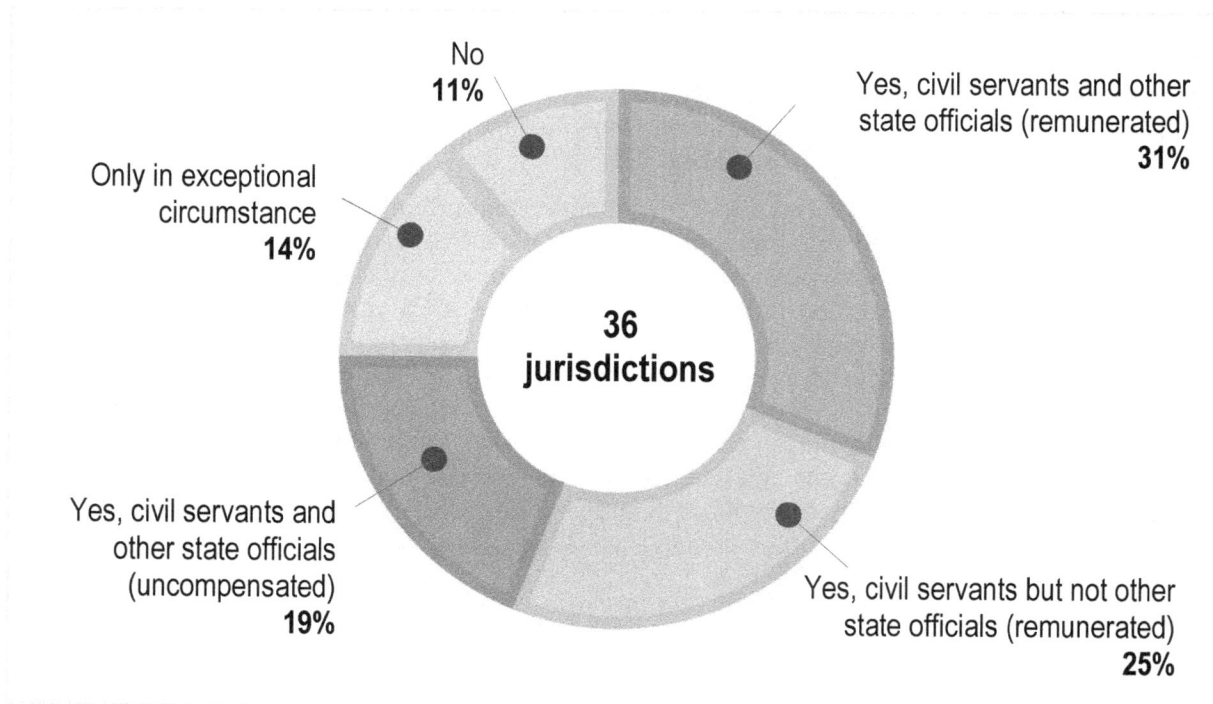

Source: Author. See Table 2.4 for details.

Table 2.4. Remuneration policies and practices of supervisory board members across 36 jurisdictions

Country	Remuneration-setting procedures	Additional provisions
Australia	The Remuneration Tribunal sets the remuneration arrangements for the nine SOE Boards including Chair, Deputy Chair (where relevant) and Directors. It seeks to determine a remuneration reference rate for directors that is commensurate with their roles and responsibilities. In setting remuneration, the Remuneration Tribunal may take into consideration information including, but not limited to, the workload and work value of the office, fees in the private sector, wage indices and other economic indices and rates set for other bodies. The Remuneration Tribunal may also consider factors such as the non-cash benefits provided, and the public interest and personal status involved in holding the office. The Department of Finance also issues its *Resource Management Guide No. 126: Commonwealth Government Business Enterprises – Governance and Oversight Guidelines* (GBE Guidelines), which contains further information regarding the appointment process and requirements for GBE Boards.	● ❖ ▲
Austria	The Ministry of Finance sets the remuneration level at its own discretion, taking in consideration the remuneration of comparable SOEs and following the directives of the manual "Equity Interest Management of the Federal Republic of Austria". In general, the remuneration is resolved by the annual general meeting. Boards are generally not consulted on their remuneration packages. The manual on "Equity Interest Management of the Federal Republic of Austria" recommends a minimum threshold of EUR 2 000 and a maximum threshold equivalent to 4% of the annual salary of the executive management for the remuneration of an ordinary board member. In addition, attendance allowances are also granted.	● ⊙ ■
Belgium	The *21 March 1991 Law on the Reform of some Public Enterprises* requires that a remuneration committee be established in each SOE. The remuneration committee provides recommendations on board remuneration levels to the General Assembly, and the latter takes the final decision in that respect.	○ ⊙ ■
Brazil	The process of defining the remuneration of SOEs' boards starts with a proposal generated within the company management. The proposal is submitted by the SOE board to the Brazilian Ministry of Economy to be further deliberated in the annual general meeting of the SOE. The role of shareholder of the Federal Union is conducted by the National Treasury Special Secretary with a delegation of the Minister of Economy. In order to subsidise the vote of the Federal Union in the annual general meeting, the National Treasury Special Secretary counts on the support of the Secretariat of Co-ordination and Governance of State-Owned Enterprises (SEST) and the National Treasury Attorney General's Office (PGFN). According to the *Board Remuneration Act 9 292/1996*, the remuneration of directors may not exceed 10% of the average remuneration of executive managers.	● ■ ▲
Bulgaria	According to the Rules for the Implementation of the Public Enterprises Act, the monthly remuneration of the members of the management and supervisory boards of public enterprises is calculated by the application of a total score determined by several variables, including the results for the reporting quarter, using the indicators and criteria (provided in Annex No. 2 of the Rules) and the established value of a score unit. However, shareholding ministries have ultimate discretion on the policies, rules and guidelines of the remuneration of the management and control bodies in SOEs from their respective portfolio, which means that they can decide to reduce the levels of remuneration by changing the value of the score unit. The terms of remuneration are included in management contracts, and the calculations themselves are carried out by each SOE. According to the Commercial Act, the remuneration of the governing bodies of SOEs is determined by the General Meeting.	● ⊙ ▲
Chile	The remuneration of board members of statutory SOEs is established in their organic laws, while for others it is either determined by the central ownership agency (SEP – Sistema de Empresas), by decrees issued by the Ministry of Finance, or by the AGM, depending on the type of SOEs. For "simplified corporations" or "sociedaded por Acciones (SpA)", remuneration is set by SEP resolutions.	●[1] ⊙ ▽
Colombia	According to Decree 2 561 de 2009, thresholds to determine the amount of board meeting allowances based on the legal monthly minimum wage were set by the Asset Committee of the MHCP in 2012. The remuneration amount is established according to the level of assets of the respective SOE, whether its purpose is to be an industrial or commercial company of the state, a mixed economy company or company in which the state has a majority shareholding, and taking into consideration their financial	● ⊙ ▽

Country	Remuneration-setting procedures	Additional provisions
	viability and the budget availability. For meetings held on the same day, only the equivalent of one session may be paid. Fees are indexed on inflation.	● ▷
Costa Rica	Remuneration policies are established in the legal framework of SOEs, either in their statutory laws or articles of incorporation. Overall, five different calculation methods exist (Box 2.3). Of note, the methods are not mutually exclusive, and sometimes do overlap for some SOEs. Regardless of the calculation method used, caps on remuneration are set by law (articles 43 and 44 of the Law for Strengthening Public Finances), but differ for public policy-oriented and commercially oriented SOEs. While board members of public policy-oriented SOEs may not receive a monthly remuneration that exceeds ten basic monthly salaries of the lowest category in the salary scale of the Public Administration, the remuneration of board members of commercially oriented SOEs cannot exceed the equivalent of 30 basic monthly salaries of the lowest category in the salary scale of the Public Administration, or approximately USD 13 260.	● ■ ▷
Croatia	The remuneration amount for the work of members of supervisory boards in majority state-owned enterprises was determined by the Government of the Republic of Croatia in 2009, and has remained in force since. Of note, remuneration levels can be reduced by the company's decision.	● ■ ◀
Czech Republic	Shareholding ministries are responsible for setting the remuneration practices for the SOEs in their portfolio, provided that they respect relevant regulations in given sectors.	⊙ ● ◀
Estonia	According to Article 80 of the State Assets Act, the Nomination Committee makes a remuneration proposal to the shareholding minister, who then approves the proposal or decides on an appropriate remuneration. There are no formal remuneration caps set by government. Prior to their appointment, board candidates are usually informed of the potential remuneration, but it is typically not negotiable. Of note, the Nomination Committee has from time to time consulted with chairpersons of the supervisory boards to get their feedback on whether the remuneration level is optimal. There is no written policy, but the aim is to be competitive with the private sector. Since the establishment of the Nomination Committee, the remuneration of SOE supervisory board members has been kept approximately at the level of comparable private companies.	○ ■ ▷
Finland	The remuneration policies for SOE boards are set by the Ownership Steering Department within the Prime Minister's office. There is an independent advisor studying the market conditions. Based on the market development, the Ownership Steering Department confirms the remuneration in the annual general meeting. Caps are set on an ad-hoc basis, as the Ownership Steering Department at the Prime Minister's office confirms the limits on a company-by-company basis before the nomination of directors.	●[2] ⊙ ■
France	The remuneration ceiling of board members is proposed by the board itself for approval by the general meeting of the companies concerned. The allocation of the pool of fees then falls within the prerogatives of the board. The compensation is calibrated taking into account the level of compensation in companies of similar size and operating in similar sectors in order to achieve harmonised compensation. The compensation of board members is capped at EUR 450 000 (gross amount) per year.	● ◆ ▷
Germany	According to the Guidelines for active management of companies in which the Federation has a holding, supervisory board members of SOEs where the Federal States hold, directly or indirectly, all of its shares and covers all or the major part of its expenses may only be reimbursed for their expenses and may at most receive an adequate allowance. For other SOEs, the AGM decides about the arrangements of the compensation, including possible attendance fees and/or possible additional compensation. Determinations concerning the "whether" and the "how" of the compensation may be laid down in the company's articles of association.	● ■ ▷[3]
Greece	For SOEs that fall under the scope of Law 3429/2005 on SOEs, board remuneration is determined by a joint decision of the Minister of Finance and the supervising Minister, and cannot exceed the cap set by Law 4354/2015 (public sector wage grid), which is equal to the monthly salary of the General Secretary of the ministry (currently equal to EUR 4 631). For SOEs which are exempt from this law, i.e. whose shares have been transferred to HCAP and which either employ more than 3 000 employees or their work cycle on company/group level exceeds 100 million euros, the Candidates Committee of the ownership agency (Hellenic Corporation of Assets and Participations – HCAP) submits a proposal for approval by the HCAP's board, taking into account the remuneration levels of similar private companies. For SOEs admitted to trading on the stock exchange, the remuneration policy is also approved by the general assembly.	● ■ ▷
Hungary	While caps on remuneration are set by law (Act 122 of 2009 on the more efficient operation of SOEs), the exact remuneration amount is decided by the annual general meeting. The ministry responsible for state asset management (NVTNM) issued a non-binding guideline for SOEs on remuneration for executive managers and board	● ⊙ ◀

Country	Remuneration-setting procedures	Additional provisions
	members, as well as a best practice on how to define the amount of remuneration for board members. According to *Act 122 of 2009*, maximum remuneration is based on the mandatory minimum wage at any given time. As the mandatory minimum wage varies year by year as defined by the government, this gives the right to shareholders to modify the remuneration amount yearly.	○ ❖ ▲ 4
Iceland	The Ministry of Finance and Economic Affairs administers the state-owned enterprises and formulates a general ownership policy for all SOEs. The company submits proposals to the owner's representative at the Annual General Meeting where the remuneration is approved.	● ☒ ▲
Ireland	The Department of Public Expenditure and Reform (DPER) is responsible for co-ordinating the determination of remuneration levels, as well as for publishing various codes guiding remuneration practices, including the *Remuneration and Superannuation Code of Practice* and the *Code of Practice for the Governance of State Bodies*. Of note, fixed remuneration levels have been set in 2010 and have remained in effect since.	● ◆ ▽
Israel	Board remuneration is determined by law. As such, it is fixed and does not depend on the company's decision or consultation with the members of the board of directors.	● ◆ ◆
Japan	The remuneration of Audit and Supervisory Board Members is usually determined after the remuneration limit (annual amount) is resolved at the General Meeting of Shareholders, and the Audit and Supervisory Board Members subsequently deliberate how to allocate remuneration within the range of the remuneration limit. Prior to its submission for approval by the AGM, the remuneration of Audit and Supervisory Board Members is also usually benchmarked against the levels of similar private counterparts.	○ ❖ ◆
Korea	According to *Article 33 of the Act on the Management of Public Institutions* and *Article 5 of the Guidelines for Remuneration for Executive Officers of Public Corporations and Quasi-governmental institutions*, the guidelines for remuneration of executive officers of a public corporation or quasi-governmental institution shall be determined by the board of directors in accordance with the guidelines for remuneration determined by the Minister of Strategy and Finance through the deliberation and resolution by the Steering Committee. Further, remuneration for non-standing auditors and non-standing directors should be capped at KRW 30 million per year, including monthly allowances or attendance allowances, etc.	● ☒ ▣
Latvia	The decision regarding the supervisory board remuneration is made during the annual general meeting, within the limits on remuneration set by law. In addition, the central ownership agency (Cross-sectoral Co-ordination Centre – CSCC) has issued *Remuneration Guidelines*, which set out best practices for establishing a methodology for calculating optimal board remuneration levels. The Guidelines state that board remuneration should be comparable to the remuneration in similar private companies, and that they should be competitive for commercially oriented SOEs. In addition to setting out remuneration policies, the CSCC also provides consultations and seminars to supervisory boards and holders of state capital shares. According to *Cabinet Regulations No.63*, the monthly remuneration of board members is linked to the average monthly salary of the previous year and multiplied with coefficients ranging from 1.5 to 3, depending on the size of the SOE.	● ⊙ ▲
Lithuania	According to *Resolution No. 1 092 of the Government of the Republic of Lithuania of 14 October 2015* (for statutory enterprises) and *Resolution No. 665 of the Government of the Republic of Lithuania of 6 June 2012* (for state-owned limited liability companies), board members of statutory enterprises are subject to an hourly pay system, which entails that board members shall fill in activity reports and their working hours shall be remunerated at the hourly rate set by the ownership entity. For board members of state-owned limited liability enterprises, the decision on the level of remuneration is taken by the general meeting of shareholders. Overall, boards themselves are not involved in setting actual remuneration of board members but may be consulted or may provide their opinion.	● ◆
Mexico	According to *Article 23 of the CFE Statutory Law*, the formalisation of the remuneration of the directors of the Federal Government, who are not public servants, as well as the independent directors, is carried out through the adoption of the determination issued by the "special committee" made up of two representatives of the Ministry of Finance and Public Credit and a representative of the Ministry of Energy. The compensation limit is set forth in the specific tabulator. In the case of PEMEX, a Special Committee comprised of two representatives of the Ministry of Finance and Public Credit and a representative of the Ministry of Energy determines the remuneration for the independent directors and the commissioner.	● ◆ ▣
Netherlands	According to the Government's SOE board remuneration policy (laid out in *section 6.7 of the 2013 Central Government Participations Policy*), the SOE board can propose	○ ☒ ▲

Country	Remuneration-setting procedures	Additional provisions
	its own remuneration practices for approval by the General Meeting of Shareholders. Of note, the Ministry of Finance and the board usually try to reach an agreement on the board proposal during informal meetings, before formalising the policy during the AGM.	
New Zealand	For *Crown company boards*, the Treasury advises the Shareholding Ministers on appropriate fees according to the Crown Company Fees Methodology, which evaluates companies under nine factors and then allocates a benchmarked points ranking. The Treasury then provides these rankings to an independent remuneration specialist, who provides comparative private sector rates. For *non-company Crown entities*, the Treasury advises the Minister on remuneration in accordance with the Cabinet Fees Framework. Board fees of *independent Crown entities* are set by the Remuneration Authority. The Shareholding Ministers annually approve a fees pool for each board, which then determines how to allocate this pool of fees. The base rate used to calculate the fee pool for directorships ranges from USD 18 000 to USD 54 500 per annum per director. The actual rate depends on a number of factors, including the size and complexity of the company and the diversity of its operations and markets, and associated risk profile.	O[5] ❖ ▲
Norway	The remuneration policies for SOE boards are set in the report to the Storting on state ownership issued by the Ministry of Trade, Fishery and Industries. However, it is up to the general meeting of each company to decide the remuneration of the board. The shareholding ministry represents the state at the general meeting. In particular, the ministry that represents the Norwegian state as owner at the general meeting will propose and vote for, or, in companies with a nomination committee, endorse, remuneration levels that are in accordance with the state ownership policy, but there are no fixed limits or fixed remuneration caps.	O ⊠ ▲
Peru	The central ownership agency (FONAFE) has the responsibility for establishing the remuneration of the directors of the companies under its scope. As such, in 2015, it established fixed remuneration amounts according to the four categories of SOEs. Overall, the average compensation that the director receives (without considering his participation in board committees) amounts to the equivalent of USD 14 400 annually.	● ⊙ ▽
Philippines	Remuneration policies of SOEs are set by the central ownership agency (GCC) in line with existing laws. Overall, the per diems, allowances, incentives, and compensation structure for the members of the Governing Boards have been set out by the GCC in 2011 according to five categories of SOEs. These levels have been maintained since 2011. For public policy-oriented SOEs, the total annual per diems and incentives that the board members may receive shall be determined by the President upon the recommendation of the central ownership agency based on individual SOEs' performance.	● ■ ▽
Portugal	Board remuneration is set according to Resolution of the Council of Ministers No. 16/2012 of 14 February 2012 and Article 29 of Decree-Law No. 71/2007 of 27 March. As such, the remuneration of non-executive directors is limited to a quarter of the remuneration established for the respective executive directors. In addition, the recruitment process for non-executive directors is the responsibility of the Public Administration Recruitment and Selection Commission (CRESAP). Non-executive directors are recruited from among persons with proven moral integrity, suitable competence and management experience and with, at least, a university degree.	● ⊙ ▲
Slovak Republic	Three subsystems exist for establishing remuneration policies, according to the legal form of SOEs and their respective share of state ownership. For **wholly owned SOEs**, the *Resolution of the Slovak Government No. 159/2011 of 2 March 2011 on the Rules of Recruitment* manages the remuneration of the state officials on the boards. However, the shareholding ministry is responsible for customising these general rules to the conditions of the respective SOE. Moreover, some internal implementation procedures and policies may also be elaborated by SOEs themselves. Remuneration itself is based on the merit and performance principles with regard to the role/position of the SOE within the national economy. The fixed remuneration component of supervisory board members is set as a multiple of the average nominal wage as calculated by the National Statistical Office. This fixed component is supplemented with another remuneration component of economic nature, reflecting the size of the SOE and its position within the national economy (including return on investment, net turnover, and number of employees). Overall, the total remuneration of board members of wholly owned SOEs may not exceed the amount equal to 10 times the average wage of the previous year. For **less than 100%-owned SOEs**, the rules for remuneration are adopted by the SOE General Meeting (the remuneration is set according to the historical remuneration reflecting the growth of the SOEs and the role/position of the SOE within the national economy). For **statutory enterprises** regulated by *Act No. 111/1990 Coll. on State Enterprise*, the monthly salary a member of the supervisory board cannot exceed five times the average wage in the national economy of the previous year.	●[6] ◆ ▲
Spain	Remuneration is approved at the general meetings of the companies respecting the caps set by the Treasury, although in companies in which the state has a majority	● ■ ▽

Country	Remuneration-setting procedures	Additional provisions
	shareholding, voting may be influenced by the general guidelines approved by the Ministry of Finance. In state-owned industrial entities, such as port companies (Ports) and railway administrators (ADIF), the Ministry of Finance has the power to set maximum limits in order to ensure the integrity and balance of the budget.	
Sweden	Board remuneration levels are proposed by the owner(s) and then formally decided by the annual general meeting. In wholly owned SOEs, board remuneration is in practice decided by the government. Ahead of the general meeting's decision on directors' fees, the Government Office carries out an analysis comparing fee levels with those paid by comparable companies (~300 listed companies, Nasdaq OMX). The fees should be competitive, but not market-leading. Following this comparative analysis, the ownership entity within the Ministry of Enterprise and Innovation makes a proposal for annual remuneration changes, which is submitted for a first approval by the Minister for Business, Industry and Innovation, and a second approval by the Prime Minister's Office. Overall, limits are usually set by the Prime Minister's office.	●[7] ◆ ▲
Switzerland	Remuneration is determined by the company based on relevant rules and regulations (including Art. 6a Loi sur le personnel de la Confédération and Ordonnance sur la rémunération et sur d'autres conditions contractuelles convenues avec les cadres du plus haut niveau hiérarchique et les membres des organes dirigeants des entreprises et des établissements de la Confédération). For companies limited by shares, the annual general meeting has the power to determine annually i) a ceiling for the total amount of the fees of the board members and the board chair (separately) and ii) to set an upper limit for the total amount of the remuneration of the Executive Board. For listed SOEs, remuneration is set according to the Ordonnance contre les rémunérations abusives dans les sociétés anonymes cotées en bourse.	○ ❖ ▲
Turkey	SOE board fees are determined by Presidential Decision No. 2393, which was drafted by the Ministry of Treasury and Finance, taking into account inputs from the relevant Ministries and the Presidency.	● ■ ▲
United Kingdom	Boards (more specifically Board Remuneration Committees) are generally responsible for benchmarking and establishing remuneration policies, which are submitted to line ministries for approval. In certain cases, secondary approval from the Chief Secretary to the Treasury may be required. While some SOEs' Articles of Association may set an upper cap on total board remuneration, there are no cross-government caps on the total remuneration amount, or the amount paid to an individual. However, if the remuneration of a non-executive director is above GBP 150k pro-rata and more than GBP 30k actual, approval from the Chief Secretary to the Treasury is required. Of note, there is recent experience of uplift to non-executive directors' fees first being recommended by the board Remuneration Committee, and then agreed by Government.	○ ◆ ▲

Note:
Do caps on remuneration exist? ● = Yes, caps exist; ○ = No caps
Can civil servants or direct state representatives serve on boards? ⊙ = civil servants and other state officials (remunerated); ■ = civil servants but not other state officials (remunerated); ◆ = civil servants and other state officials (uncompensated); ❖ = only in exceptional circumstances; ⊠ = No.
On remuneration components: ▲ = fixed fees; ▽ = board meeting allowances; ■ = combination of both.
[1] In **Chile**, caps on remuneration exist for statutory SOEs only.
[2] In **Finland**, caps are set on an ad-hoc basis.
[3] In **Germany**, fixed fees and combinations of both fixed fees and allowances are possible for board members of SOEs, albeit only if the public sector is **not** the sole shareholder in the equity of the company, either directly or indirectly, and the company's expenditures are **not** borne wholly or to a significant extent by the public sector.
[4] In **Iceland**, while fixed fees are granted to the board members of most SOEs, board meeting allowances may be granted as well to the board member of small SOEs only.
[5] In **New Zealand**, limits are set on a case-by-case basis.
[6] In the **Slovak Republic**, caps on board remuneration exist for wholly owned SOEs and statutory SOEs.
[7] In **Sweden**, caps are set on an ad-hoc basis.
Source: Author, based on questionnaire responses and desk research.

2.4. Transparency and disclosure practices

The *SOE Guidelines* state that SOEs should ensure high levels of transparency regarding the remuneration of board members and key executives. In all but three of the surveyed countries, SOEs are required to disclose information on the remuneration levels of board members to the general public, albeit with varying levels of granularity: 22 countries require SOEs to do so for individual members, while they are required do so for the board as a whole in 11 countries (Figure 2.7). In **Switzerland**, SOEs are required to disclose individual remuneration levels for the chair of the board only, and an aggregate disclosure for the remuneration of the board as a whole. Some countries report that SOEs are also required to disclose the remuneration policy (**Greece**, **Hungary**, **Korea**, the **Netherlands**, **New Zealand**, **Philippines**, **United Kingdom**).[1]

2.4.1. Medium for disclosure

The medium for such disclosures also varies across countries. While in a majority of countries, SOEs mainly release this information in their annual reports, which are subsequently made publicly available on their websites, some countries require SOEs to disclose this information in a dedicated remuneration report[2] (**Belgium**, **Sweden**). Some countries also display interesting venues for disclosure by SOEs. For instance, in **Brazil**, SOEs make this information publicly available on a dedicated webpage of their websites, and in **Norway**, the state expects SOEs to publish on their webpage the minutes from the general meeting with information regarding the remuneration decided by the general meeting, including fixed remuneration and remuneration for committee membership. In addition, the *Accounting Act* requires all companies that are not small to disclose the aggregate salary provided to the board. From 2023, most SOEs (including unlisted entities) will be required to publish an annual remuneration report. In **Sweden**, this information is also made public through the nomination decision made by government, and through the AGM minutes which are made public on companies' webpages under the corporate governance section.

2.4.2. "Proactive" and "reactive" disclosure

While in the majority of surveyed countries, SOEs are required to "proactively" disclose this information, in some countries, SOEs that are subject to the transparency act disclose this information only when requested (e.g. **Mexico**, **Costa Rica**, the **Slovak Republic**). However, in the **Slovak Republic**, some cases have been brought before the courts claiming that SOEs do not qualify as "public entities" subject to the transparency act, and thus do not have such a duty.

2.4.3. Comparing requirements for listed and non-listed SOEs

In terms of how SOEs fare against listed companies' practices, it is interesting to note that in some countries, more stringent provisions exist for unlisted SOEs than for listed SOEs (**Brazil**, the **Czech Republic**), while in other countries, provisions are more restrictive for listed SOEs than for unlisted SOEs (**Croatia**, **Israel**). In some countries, the same requirements apply to both listed and unlisted SOEs indifferently (**Lithuania**, **Sweden**). In the **Netherlands**, the Ministry of Finance requests SOEs to abide by a practice that is mandatory for listed companies, and which entails publishing a compliance report describing how the remuneration policy has been implemented.

Figure 2.7. Disclosure practices by SOEs and the state regarding board remuneration levels

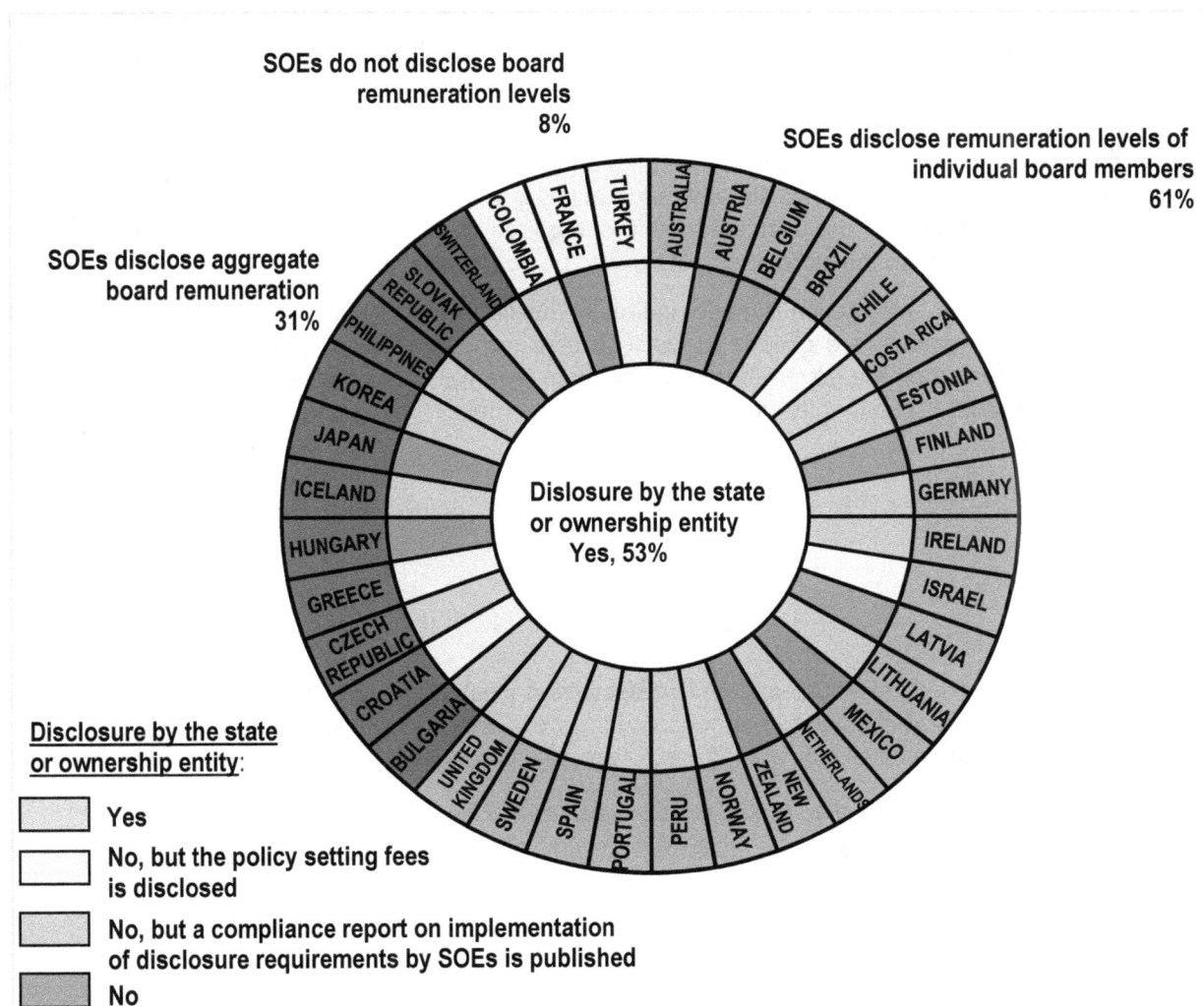

SOEs do not disclose board remuneration levels
8%

SOEs disclose remuneration levels of individual board members
61%

SOEs disclose aggregate board remuneration
31%

Dislosure by the state or ownership entity
Yes, 53%

Disclosure by the state or ownership entity:

- [ ] Yes
- [ ] No, but the policy setting fees is disclosed
- [ ] No, but a compliance report on implementation of disclosure requirements by SOEs is published
- [ ] No

Source: Author, based on questionnaire responses and desk research.

2.4.4. Disclosure practices by the state or ownership entity

On average, individual SOEs disclose board remuneration information of greater granularity than the state. However, in **Iceland**, the opposite is true with the government being more transparent than individual SOEs regarding the level of granularity of information disclosed. While SOEs disclose information on the remuneration of the board as a whole in their annual reports, the ministry publishes information about the board members, name, gender balance for each board and monthly remuneration for individual board members on the Ministry's website.[3]

In some countries, a central online portal aggregating all remuneration information by all SOEs in the state's portfolio has been set up either by central government (**Australia**,[4] **Korea**[5]), the ownership entity (**Portugal**[6]) or the central ownership agency (**Peru**[7]), making this information readily accessible. In **Bulgaria**, the ownership agency discloses information on the remuneration of the management and control bodies of large public enterprises only in its annual aggregate report, which is made publicly available on the agency's website.

While in some countries, the state does not "proactively" publish information about board remuneration levels, it publishes a compliance report on the implementation of disclosure requirements by SOEs. For instance, in **Costa Rica**, the Presidential Advisory Unit on State Ownership does disclose whether specific SOEs are complying with their responsibility to publish the required board and management remuneration information, as part of the analysis included in the annual State Ownership's Aggregate Report on SOEs.

The state does not publish information on board remuneration in 17 of the 36 surveyed countries. In some cases, this is explained by the fact that it is deemed unnecessary, as remuneration levels are harmonised or capped, and these thresholds are already made public in the legal frameworks of SOEs (e.g. **Croatia**, **Israel**, **Turkey**), or because the company itself is required to publish granular information on board members' remuneration, so the state does not have to do so (**Hungary**).

In other cases however, information is made "indirectly" available by the state, because as public officials, supervisory board members are obliged to disclose their remuneration, and such disclosures are then made publicly available on the government's online state revenue service database (**Latvia**). Likewise in the **Slovak Republic**, "public officials" are required to make their remuneration available on the parliament's website.

References

Afanador, S., A. Bernal and A. Oneto (2017), "Efectividad y estructura de los directorios de las empresas de propiedad estatal en América Latina y el Caribe", *Políticas públicas y transformación productiva*, Vol. 26, http://scioteca.caf.com/handle/123456789/1018. [1]

Australian Post (2021), *Australian Postal Corporation Annual Report 2019-20*, https://www.transparency.gov.au/annual-reports/australian-postal-corporation/reporting-year/2019-20-99. [6]

European Commission (2016), *State-Owned Enterprises in the EU: Lessons Learnt and Ways Forward in a Post-Crisis Context*, https://ec.europa.eu/info/publications/economy-finance/state-owned-enterprises-eu-lessons-learnt-and-ways-forward-post-crisis-context_en. [7]

Focus Orange (2019), *EVALUATIE COMMISSARISSENBELONING BIJ STAATSDEELNEMINGEN*, https://www.rijksoverheid.nl/binaries/rijksoverheid/documenten/kamerstukken/2021/01/29/evaluatie-commissarisbeloningen/evaluatie-commissarisbeloningen.pdf. [2]

IBP (2014), *Transparency of State-Owned Enterprises in South Korea*, https://www.internationalbudget.org/wp-content/uploads/Hidden-Corners-South-Korea.pdf. [9]

IDB (2016), *State-owned enterprise management: advantages of centralized models*, https://publications.iadb.org/publications/english/document/State-owned-Enterprise-Management-Advantages-of-Centralized-Models.pdf. [11]

IMF (2017), *State-Owned Enterprises in Emerging Europe: The Good, the Bad, and the Ugly*, https://www.imf.org/en/Publications/WP/Issues/2017/10/30/State-Owned-Enterprises-in-Emerging-Europe-The-Good-the-Bad-and-the-Ugly-45181. [15]

IMF/ERBD (2019), *Reassessing the Role of State-Owned Enterprises in Central, Eastern, and Southeastern Europe*, https://www.imf.org/en/Publications/Departmental-Papers-Policy-Papers/Issues/2019/06/17/Reassessing-the-Role-of-State-Owned-Enterprises-in-Central-Eastern-and-Southeastern-Europe-46859. [12]

Norwegian government (2019), *Report to the Storting*, https://www.regjeringen.no/en/dokumenter/meld.-st.-8-20192020/id2678758/. [3]

Norwegian Institute of Directors (2019), *Board Remuneration Survey: listed and State-owned companies*. [16]

OECD (2022), *Monitoring the Performance of State-Owned Enterprises: Good Practice Guide for Annual Aggregate Reporting*, https://www.oecd.org/corporate/ca/Monitoring-performance-state-owned-enterprises-good-practice-guide-annual-aggregate-reporting-2022.pdf. [10]

OECD (2021), *Ownership and Governance of State-Owned Enterprises: A Compendium of National Practices*, https://www.oecd.org/corporate/ownership-and-governance-of-state-owned-enterprises-a-compendium-of-national-practices.htm. [4]

OECD (2020), *Implementing the OECD Guidelines on Corporate Governance of State-Owned Enterprises: Review of Recent Developments*, OECD Publishing, Paris, https://doi.org/10.1787/4caa0c3b-en. [22]

OECD (2020), *OECD Review of the Corporate Governance of State-Owned Enterprises: Brazil*, http://www.oecd.org/corporate/soe-review-brazil.htm. [17]

OECD (2020), *Transparency and Disclosure Practices of State-Owned Enterprises and their Owners*, OECD Publishing, Paris, http://www.oecd.org/corporate/transparency-disclosure-practices-soes. [8]

OECD (2018), *Ownership and Governance of State-Owned Enterprises: A Compendium of National Practices*, https://www.oecd.org/corporate/ca/Ownership-and-Governance-of-State-Owned-Enterprises-A-Compendium-of-National-Practices.pdf. [18]

OECD (2015), *OECD Guidelines on Corporate Governance of State-Owned Enterprises*, https://www.oecd.org/corporate/guidelines-corporate-governance-soes.htm. [21]

OECD (2015), *OECD Review of the Corporate Governance of State-Owned Enterprises in Latvia*, https://www.oecd.org/daf/ca/oecd-review-corporate-governance-soe-latvia.htm. [19]

OECD (2015), *OECD Review of the Corporate Governance of State-Owned Enterprises in Lithuania*, https://www.oecd.org/countries/lithuania/oecd-review-corporate-governance-soe-lithuania.htm. [20]

OECD (2011), *Corporate Governance of State-Owned Enterprises: Change and Reform in OECD Countries since 2005*, OECD Publishing, Paris, https://doi.org/10.1787/9789264119529-en. [13]

World Bank (2016), *International experience in governance of state-owned enterprises and parastatals*. [5]

World Bank (2014), *Tendencias del Gobierno Corporativo de las empresas publicas en América Latina : Tendencias y Casos de Países*, https://openknowledge.worldbank.org/handle/10986/19983?locale-attribute=es. [14]

Notes

[1] In **Greece**, for SOEs in the portfolio of the Ministry of Finance, monthly allowances range between EUR 200 to EUR 800.

[2] The study indicates that from the sample of five countries where SOEs use board meeting attendance allowances as the method of board remuneration (15 companies, including all participating Costa Rican SOEs), the allowance amount stands between USD 74 and USD 995, for an average monthly board meeting attendance allowance of USD 467.

[3] However, in **Chile**, in port state companies the vice president earns the same as any other board member.

[4] In **Estonia**, while the remuneration of the chair of the supervisory board is typically double the amount of a regular supervisory board member remuneration, in some instances the difference is smaller.

[5] In **Costa Rica**, SOEs with an Executive President include: ICE, INS, AyA, INCOP, JAPDEVA, INCOFER, FANAL. SOEs with non-executive chairs include: JPS, BCR, BNCR, RECOPE S.A., Costa Rican Mail Service S.A., and SINART S.A.

[6] For instance, in **Chile**, the chair of the board committee of commercially oriented SOEs and its members receive all the same allowance for attending board meetings, except for ENAP and CODELCO where remuneration levels differ. Likewise, in **Colombia**, the Assets Committee set the same threshold of payment for board and committee meetings in 2013. As such, approximately 70% of the majority-owned SOEs pay the same amount to board members and board committee members. In **Costa Rica**, attendance allowances of board committee meetings are similar for the committee chair and the rest of its members, and do not present significant variations across SOEs.

[7] Of note, it may be inferred that these variables are intertwined insofar as countries with mainly commercial SOEs might have adopted a centralised ownership model, and require boards to be comprised of a majority of independent members appointed according to strict selection criteria. Details on ownership models are provided in (OECD, 2021[4]).

[8] As of July 2021, the fixed component of a congressperson's monthly remuneration is USD 4.761. The source data can be found at: http://www.asamblea.go.cr/opendata.

[9] These officials include the President of the Republic; Ministers of State and Undersecretaries; Intendants and Superior Heads of Service; and those performing functions classified as critical.

[1] Of note, in **France**, although SOEs are not required to disclose information on remuneration levels to the general public, they usually do publish information on remuneration levels of the board as a whole (after it has been approved by the AGM and shareholders) and on the remuneration policy in their annual reports.

[2] As required by the EU Directive: https://ec.europa.eu/info/sites/default/files/rrg_draft_21012019.pdf.

[3] https://www.stjornarradid.is/verkefni/rekstur-og-eignir-rikisins/felog-i-eigu-rikisins/

[4] https://www.transparency.gov.au

[5] https://www.alio.go.kr/

[6] http://www.dgtf.pt/sector-empresarial-do-estado-see/informacao-sobre-as-empresas

[7] https://www.fonafe.gob.pe/centrocorporativo/buengobiernocorporativo

3 Remuneration schemes applicable to executive management of SOEs

This chapter takes stock of policies and practices underpinning the remuneration of executive managers of SOEs across countries. It takes stock of executive remuneration levels and pay packages, and explores the extent to which the state as an owner influences the board of directors' autonomy to decide on managerial remuneration and incentives. The chapter also presents good transparency and disclosure practices.

3.1. Introduction

Managerial remuneration in SOEs straddles the spheres of corporate and public sector governance. On one hand, adequate remuneration levels are crucial for attracting competent executive managers in SOEs and to incentivise them in accordance with the interests of the owners. On the other hand, for political and societal reasons care must be taken to avoid setting these at a level perceived by the general public as being too high. The *SOE Guidelines* imply that care should be taken to ensure that the state owners do not infringe on the boards' role in determining managerial salaries. If the state wishes to influence this, general rules should be established and/or owners' expectations regarding remuneration should be communicated to the boards through the usual channels of control.

Main findings

Remuneration levels, policies and practices

- Practices regarding executive remuneration vary significantly across countries. In countries facing specific political or fiscal constraints, remuneration is generally prescribed by law or by separate government decision, with levels standing (sometimes significantly) below the average of SOEs in other countries, as well as lower than market levels in the domestic economy. On the other hand, in countries where remuneration is set at the full discretion of the board, levels are generally higher – sometimes explicitly based on private sector benchmarks.

- Regardless of the way in which remuneration policies are established, average CEO remuneration is twice as high in commercially oriented SOEs as in public policy-oriented SOEs, except in countries where levels are set by law. In many countries, the disparity between remuneration levels of CEOs of large SOEs and small SOEs is also significant. Some outliers exist in some sectors, for instance the air transport sector, where caps may have been derogated in order to accommodate generally high sectoral pay levels. Unsurprisingly, the remuneration of the CEO is generally higher than the remuneration of other executive managers. In some cases, the differences actually seem to be smaller than might have been expected in the private sector.

- The majority of countries hire executive managers on fixed-term contracts, while only eight countries exclusively hire executive managers – including both the CEO and other members of the management board – on continuous contracts with terms for termination, like in the private sector. In these countries, the boards also set remuneration levels at their full discretion, similar to private sector practices. In six countries, both contractual relationships are possible.

Remuneration components

- Pay packages of executive managers usually include an annual fixed salary (which can be based on the consumer price index or set as a multiple of the average nominal wage), allowances, fringe benefits and payments to the pension plan, and can also include severance payments. Stock options are not allowed in all but two countries.

- In all but five of the surveyed countries, executive managers' pay packages also include a performance-based component, which is capped by the government owner in more than half of surveyed countries, either at the absolute level (in around one-fifth of countries), or at a percentage of the fixed remuneration component (in around four-fifths of countries).

- While limited information is available regarding how performance is benchmarked since these key performance indicators are mostly set at the full discretion of the board (sometimes upon recommendations of the remuneration committee) and not by government – and thus vary across companies, many countries mention that performance is benchmarked against profitability relative to other companies and compared to the previous year. In many countries, performance of the CEO is also benchmarked against both corporate (SOE-level) and individual performance indicators. Financial and non-financial indicators can be both qualitative and quantitative.

Transparency and disclosure practices

- In all but two countries, SOEs are required to disclose information on the remuneration levels of executive managers to the general public, along with the remuneration policy including details of the bonus schemes in many countries. In some countries, disclosure requirements apply only for the remuneration of the CEO and/or only in the case of listed companies. In some countries, some SOEs also disclose disaggregated information on the fixed and variable remuneration components. While SOEs are mainly required to disclose this information in their annual reports or websites, a separate remuneration report is required to be prepared by the company or the remuneration committee in two countries.

- By contrast, the state or ownership entity does not disclose information on executive remuneration in almost half of the surveyed countries, mainly because individual SOEs are already required to do so. In the 15 countries where the government does disclose granular information, this is mainly done through a central government portal, or the government or ownership entity's annual report on SOEs.

3.2. Actual remuneration levels of executive managers according to SOE corporate characteristics

Similar to trends regarding board remuneration, CEOs of public policy-oriented SOEs receive lower annual nominal compensation (USD 137 452 on average, representing approximately 5 times the amount of average annual national wages of production workers) than CEOs of commercially oriented SOEs (USD 201 635 on average, representing almost seven times the amount of the average annual national wages of production workers). **Croatia** and **Turkey** stand as exceptions, as remuneration levels are prescribed by law (Figure 3.1). The three countries which set the highest annual nominal wages for CEOs of commercially oriented SOEs in absolute terms (**New Zealand**, **Sweden**, **Finland**) also remain above average when remuneration levels are captured as a multiple of average annual national wages (Figure 3.2).

Relatively high remuneration levels in **New Zealand** can be explained by the fact that unlike other countries in the figure, data includes both fixed and variable remuneration components, in addition to the fact that bonuses granted to executive managers of commercially oriented SOEs are not capped, and defined at the full discretion of the board. In **Sweden**, although remuneration levels are relatively high compared to other countries, evidence suggests that levels are above medium market levels for small SOEs but below market levels for large SOEs (Swedish Government, 2021[1]). This may be due to the fact that pay packages of executive managers do not include a performance-related component. Anecdotal evidence also suggests that this has hampered recruitment, with CEO prospects turning down offers in some instances.

Figure 3.1. Average annual remuneration of CEOs of SOEs (fixed remuneration only, in USD as of 2020)

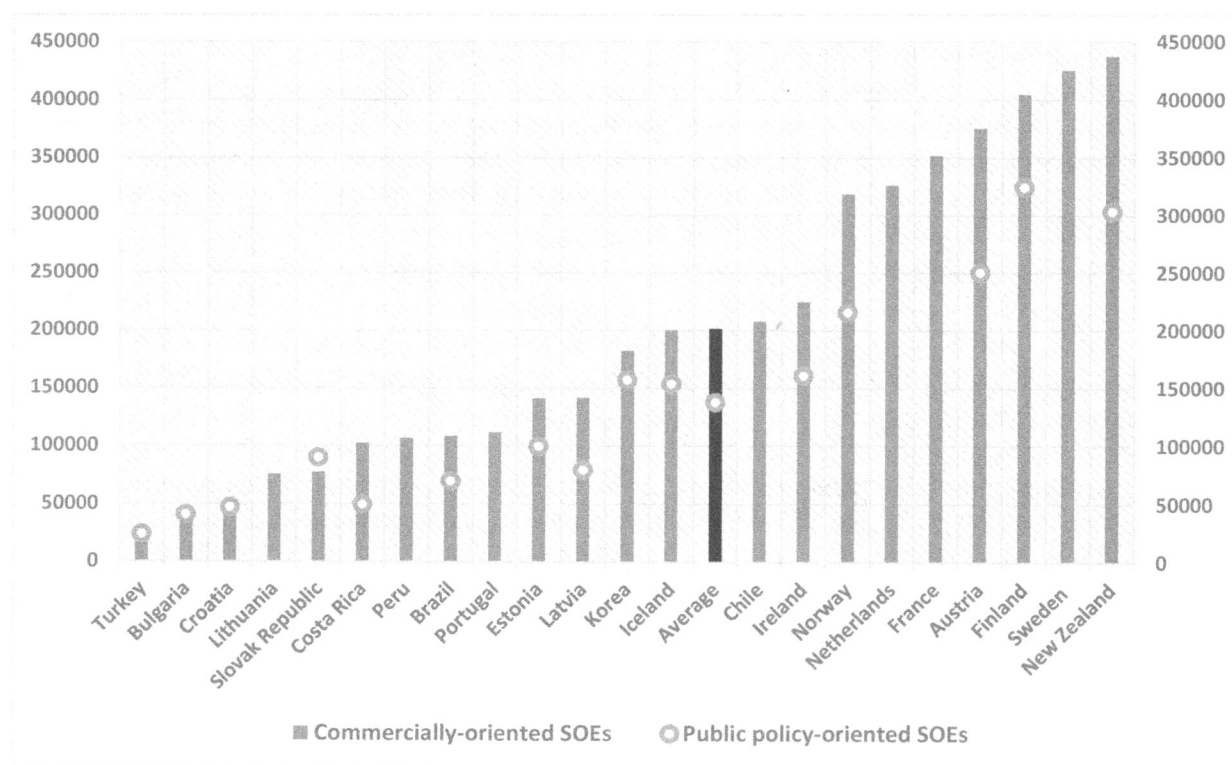

■ Commercially-oriented SOEs   ○ Public policy-oriented SOEs

Note: Data covers executive remuneration of SOEs with a state shareholding of at least 50%, which are not listed on the stock exchange, except for **Chile** where data includes one listed SOE (ZOFRI), albeit with remuneration levels similar to those of non-listed SOEs. Data includes fixed remuneration only, except for **Brazil, Estonia, Finland, Latvia**, the **Netherlands** and **New Zealand** where both fixed and variable remuneration are included. In **Chile, France, the Netherlands, Peru, Portugal** and **Sweden**, all SOEs are classified as commercially oriented. See Annex C for details.
Source: Author, based on questionnaire responses, and calculations using the OECD database (https://data.oecd.org/earnwage/average-wages.htm) and ILOSTAT database (https://ilostat.ilo.org/topics/wages/).

Similar to trends on board remuneration, high executive remuneration levels displayed as a percentage of average annual national wages in **Brazil** and **Peru** can likely be explained by low average nominal wages in these countries and the need to set remuneration levels at a high threshold in order for them to remain competitive with private sector peers. Besides, in **Brazil**, unlike other countries in the figure, data includes both the fixed and variable remuneration components. The latter can vary from 16% to 100% of the fixed remuneration depending on the company size and sector of operation.

In many countries, the disparity between remuneration levels of CEOs of large SOEs and small SOEs is also significant. For instance, CEO remuneration of large SOEs is equal to 3.6 times the remuneration amount of CEOs of small SOEs in **Austria**, 5.2 times the amount in **Latvia**, and 5.6 times in the **Netherlands**. This may be due to outliers in the air transport sector. For instance, in **New Zealand**, the remuneration of the CEO of one large commercially oriented SOE amounts to NZD 4 500 000. Other countries report that higher remuneration tends to be offered to executives of SOEs operating in the financial sector (**Brazil, Colombia, Iceland, Norway, United Kingdom**), energy sector (**Brazil, Colombia**, the **Czech Republic, Greece, New Zealand**), water sector (**Greece**) and health sector (**Portugal**). These cases may be explained by the fact that caps may have been derogated in order to accommodate generally high sectoral pay levels.

While limited data is available on the remuneration levels of chief financial officers (CFOs) and chief operating officers (COOs) across countries, evidence suggests that the remuneration of CEOs is generally higher than the remuneration of other executive managers, albeit not significantly in most cases.

Figure 3.2. Average annual remuneration of CEOs of SOEs (fixed remuneration only, as a multiple of average annual national wages)

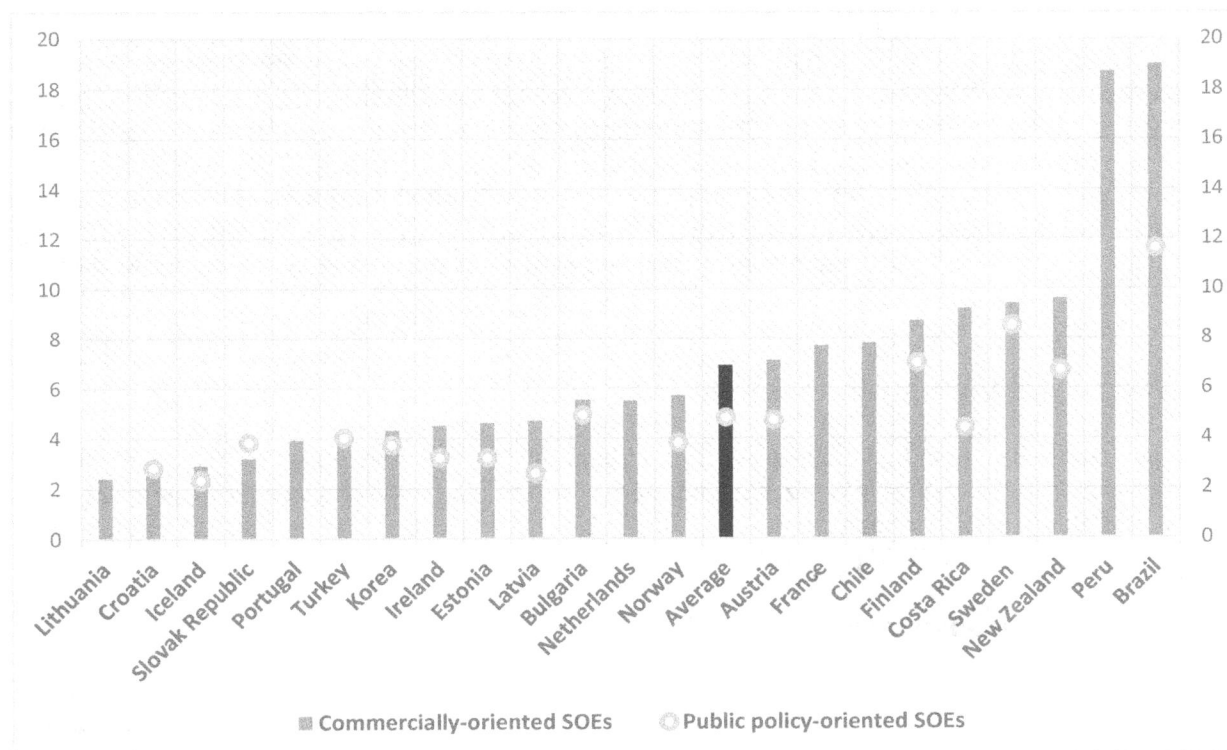

Note: Data covers executive remuneration of SOEs with a state shareholding of at least 50%, which are not listed on the stock exchange, except for **Chile** where data includes one listed SOE (ZOFRI), albeit with remuneration levels similar to those of non-listed SOEs. Data includes fixed remuneration only, except for **Brazil, Estonia, Finland, Latvia,** the **Netherlands** and **New Zealand** where both fixed and variable remuneration are included. In **Chile, France, the Netherlands, Peru, Portugal** and **Sweden,** all SOEs are classified as commercially oriented. See Annex C for details.
Source: Author, based on questionnaire responses, and calculations using the OECD database (https://data.oecd.org/earnwage/average-wages.htm) and ILOSTAT database (https://ilostat.ilo.org/topics/wages/).

In terms of comparison with private sector levels, some countries report that the remuneration of executives is comparable to private sector peers, especially in countries where the board is responsible for setting remuneration levels – sometimes based on private sector benchmarks (**Estonia, Finland, New Zealand, Norway, the Slovak Republic, United Kingdom**), or where it is provided by cabinet decision that remuneration levels must correspond to the first quartile of the market (**Chile**). However, similar to the remuneration levels of board members, many countries also report that the remuneration of executive managers stands below market levels (**Costa Rica, Croatia, France, Greece, Ireland, Israel, Latvia, Spain**) especially for executives of medium-sized and small SOEs (**Iceland, Lithuania**).

While this is mainly due to government-imposed caps on remuneration, some countries report that these have hampered recruitment. For instance, in **Costa Rica,** freezes of chief executive wages and the establishment of remuneration caps have reportedly "degraded" the institutional salary scale in absolute terms and created "inverted" gaps between senior managers and the rest of the administration, while also hampering recruitment by preventing SOEs from using market research-based remuneration practices. In **Greece**, the lower remuneration levels of executives of SOEs subjected to remuneration caps implemented during the 2008 global financial crisis reportedly hampers recruitment. As such, differentiated remuneration rules for executives of "large" SOEs (with more than 3 000 employees and EUR 100 million of annual turnover) were introduced in 2015 in order to facilitate the recruitment of qualified professionals. In **Belgium**, it is reported that the cap on the basic remuneration of SOEs' CEOs has led some executives to leave the company when it was introduced.

On the other hand, uncapped and "competitive" remuneration levels of executive managers can be perceived as being unreasonably high, and thus can spur public controversy. For instance, in **Norway**, media coverage of SOEs focuses on remuneration levels of executives being too high. In **Lithuania**, although remuneration levels of SOEs' CEOs are moderate compared to market levels, the remuneration levels of senior civil servants are usually lower than those of the CEOs of large and medium-sized SOEs, which are thus perceived as excessively high. Likewise, in the **United Kingdom**, although remuneration is well below industry equivalents, senior pay is often very high compared to the average national wage, resulting in remuneration being often subject to public scrutiny and controversy, especially following the award of large bonuses.

3.3. Remuneration policies and practices

The *SOE Guidelines* state that the remuneration of both SOE boards and executive management should be aligned with the long-term interest of the enterprise. Concerning the executive management, the *SOE Guidelines* further offer that boards should "decide, subject to applicable rules established by the state, on the compensation of the CEO" (annotations to Chapter VII, point B).

3.3.1. Remuneration models

In 16 of the 34 surveyed countries with available information, remuneration policies and levels applicable to executive managers are set by the boards, either at their full discretion (in nine countries), or within overall limits set by government (in seven countries). In three of these countries, while the remuneration of the CEO is decided by the board, the remuneration levels of the rest of the executive managers are either decided by the CEO (**Norway**,[1] **Sweden**), or decided by the board based on the CEO's proposal (**United Kingdom**).

In another seven countries, remuneration is proposed by the boards and submitted to the AGM for approval on the limits. In some of these countries, after limits have been set, the supervisory board decides in a discretionary manner on the actual remuneration levels of the members of the executive board (**France**, **Japan**, the **Netherlands**). On the other hand, in nine of the surveyed countries, remuneration levels of executive managers are either set by law, or by the government against public sector wage grids (Figure 3.3). It should be noted that some countries fall into several categories, as different policies and practices apply to SOEs depending on their corporate form, share of state ownership and/or commercial and non-commercial orientation (**Austria**, **Colombia**, **Costa Rica**, **Greece**, **Ireland**, **Switzerland**). Detailed information on individual national practices is provided in Table 3.3.

Overall, the remuneration committee does systematically play, or can play, a role in setting the remuneration levels of executive managers in 14 of the surveyed countries, mainly including those where the remuneration levels are set by the board.

Figure 3.3. Remuneration policies and practices for executive managers of SOEs

How are remuneration levels of executive managers established?

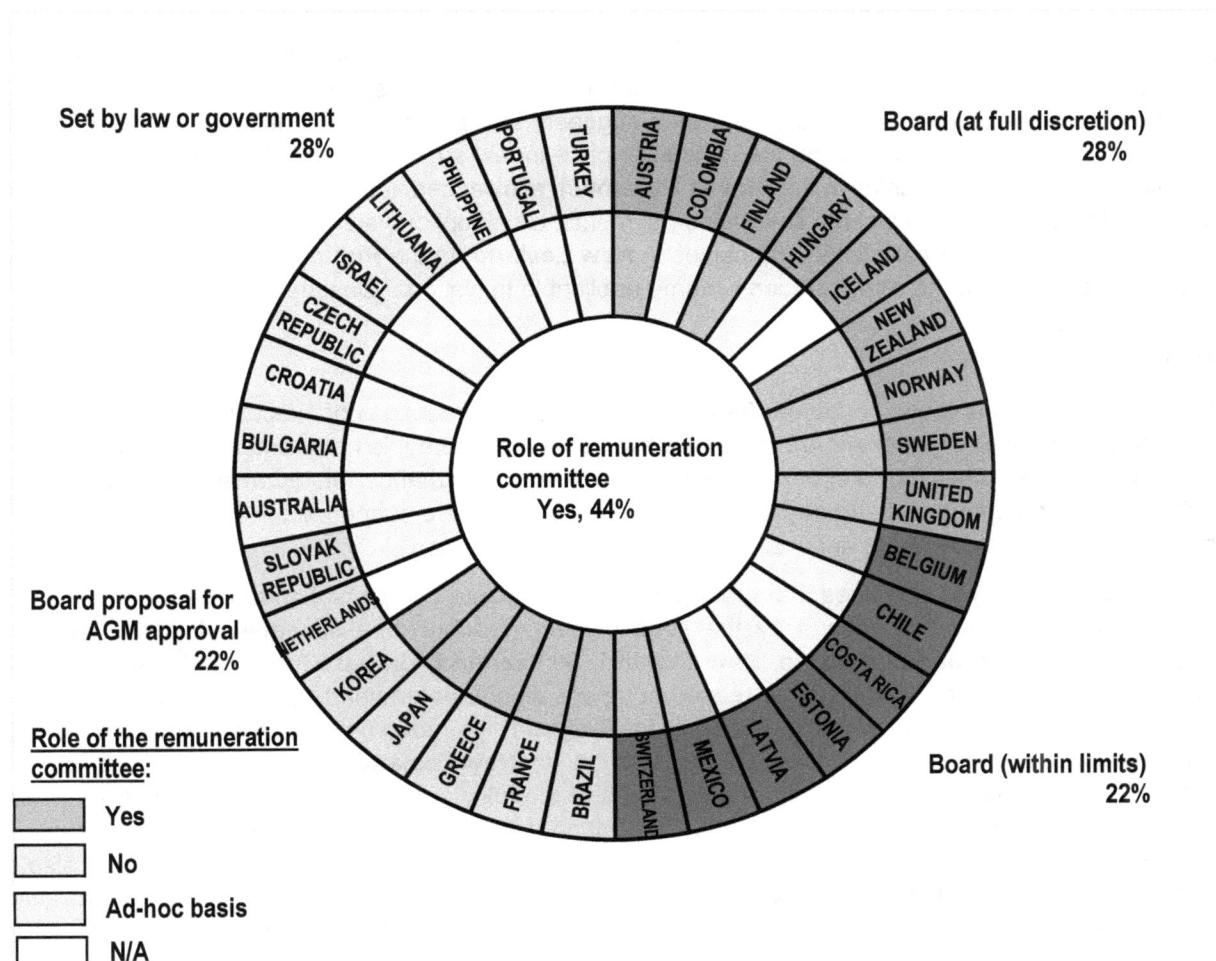

Note: Data unavailable for Peru and Spain. In Germany and Ireland, processes respectively differ according to the corporate form of SOEs and their orientation. See Table 3.3 for details.
Source: Author, based on questionnaire responses and desk research.

3.3.2. Contractual relationships of executive managers

The majority of countries hire executive managers on fixed-term contracts, while only eight countries exclusively hire executive managers – including both the CEO and other members of the management board – on continuous contracts with terms for termination, like in the private sector. In these countries, the boards also set remuneration levels at their full discretion, similar to private sector practices. In six countries, both contractual relationships are possible. For instance, in **Costa Rica**, **Ireland** and the **Slovak Republic**, CEOs are hired on fixed-term contracts, but the rest of the executive managers are offered continuous contracts with terms for termination (Table 3.3).

3.3.3. Remuneration components

The *SOE Guidelines* state that boards "should ensure that the CEO's remuneration is tied to performance and duly disclosed". They further posit that "compensation packages for senior executives should be competitive, but care should be taken not to incentivise management in a way inconsistent with the long term interest of the enterprise and its owners. The introduction of malus and claw-back provisions is considered a good practice..." (annotations to Chapter VII, point B). This effectively recommends the inclusion of a performance-related element in executive managers' pay packages.

Overall, in almost all countries, the remuneration packages of SOE executive managers include a performance-based component. While limited information is available regarding the other components of pay packages of executive managers, evidence suggests that pay packages usually include an annual fixed salary (which can be based on the consumer price index, such as in **Israel**, or as a multiple of the average nominal wage, such as in the **Slovak Republic**), allowances, fringe benefits and payments to the pension plan, and can also include severance payments. Stock options are usually not allowed, except in **Switzerland**, and for partially listed companies in **New Zealand**. In the **Philippines**, executive managers of SOEs are subject to the remuneration scheme applicable to National Government Agencies.

Variable remuneration

In almost all of the surveyed countries (85%), the remuneration packages of executive managers include a performance-based component. In four of the five countries where it is not granted (**Hungary**, **Iceland**, **Sweden**, **Turkey**), other forms of benefits exist. In **Ireland**, performance-related awards (PRAs) granted to CEOs of both commercial and non-commercial state bodies were suspended in 2009 in the context of the global economic downturn, and have not been reintroduced since.

Among the 29 surveyed countries that grant performance-related compensation to executive managers, this variable component is capped by the state owner in all but nine countries (**Austria**, **Belgium**, **Costa Rica**, **Croatia**, **Japan**, **Mexico**, **New Zealand**, **Switzerland**, **United Kingdom**). In **Austria**, while there are no formal caps, performance-related compensation is determined by the chair of the board in co-ordination with the shareholding ministry. In **Belgium**, no government caps exist, but variable remuneration can be capped at the SOEs' discretion. In **New Zealand**, while there are not caps for commercially oriented SOEs – which are determined at the full discretion of the board – no discretionary bonuses are granted to CEOs of public policy-oriented SOEs. In **Switzerland**, while no caps on remuneration currently exist, the issue is a subject of ongoing debates in parliament.[2] It should also be noted that in **Costa Rica** and **Croatia**, only two SOEs in each country pay performance-related compensation to executives, as executive remuneration in these countries is subject to a unified salary system set by law.

Among the 20 countries that cap performance-related compensation, one-third cap it at the absolute level, while the remaining 70% cap it at a percentage of the fixed remuneration (Figure 3.4). Overall, different approaches exist across countries for capping performance-based compensation (Table 3.1).

Figure 3.4. Performance-related remuneration component of executive managers of SOE

Note: Information unavailable for Peru and Spain.
Source: Author, based on questionnaire responses.

Table 3.1. Selected approaches for capping performance-related compensation of executives of SOEs

Country	Provisions
Brazil	Variable remuneration is paid to executive managers of non-dependent SOEs only, and is only granted if the company achieves a certain level of net profit.
Colombia	While variable remuneration can be capped either way, the performance-related compensation of public officials must be capped at a percentage of the fixed remuneration according to *Decree 304 of 2020*.
Czech Republic	In addition to the cap on performance-related compensation, the application of the competitive clause and severance payment – if granted – should in total not exceed six times the average monthly earnings.
Finland	The government resolution on the state ownership policy sets clear limits for the bonuses, which vary according to company categories, including a) listed or major commercial companies, b) small and medium-sized commercial companies and c) special assignment companies.
Korea	According to Article 7 of the *Guidelines for Remuneration for Executive Officers of Public Corporations and Quasi-governmental institutions*, the performance-based bonuses for management performance evaluation of the head of public corporations should be capped at 120% of the basic annual salary of the preceding year.
Latvia	The annual bonus should not exceed twice the amount of the monthly salary of the previous year. In addition, the remuneration of the other management board members is capped at 90% of the remuneration of the CEO.
Lithuania	According to the *Remuneration Resolution*, the variable component of the monthly salary of the executive of the enterprise cannot exceed 50% of the fixed component. Executive managers can also be awarded with an annual bonus from the profit of the enterprise, which cannot exceed the amount of four fixed remuneration components.
Netherlands	The variable component is capped at 20% of the fixed component.
Norway	According to the state's *Guidelines for executive remuneration in SOEs*, the government does not support bonuses exceeding 50% of the fixed annual salary. However, in listed companies, the government may support schemes where the combined bonus and stock related schemes does not exceed 80% of the fixed annual salary.
Philippines	The performance-based bonus (PBB) rates applicable to executive managers are determined by Section 6.2.1. of the *GCG M.C. No. 2019-02 on the Interim Performance-Based Bonus*. The rates of the PBB should be based on the performance of the individual executive manager, with the rates of incentives set as a multiple of the individual's monthly basic salary (MBS) of the applicable year.
Slovak Republic	While the variable remuneration of executives of wholly-owned SOEs is capped at 50% of their fixed remuneration, the variable compensation of executives of statutory enterprises is capped at both an absolute level and at a percentage of the disposable profit of the enterprises. In particular, the monthly salary of a CEO of a statutory enterprise cannot exceed eight times the average wage in the national economy for the previous year, and the annual remuneration (including share on profit) cannot exceed 10% of the disposable profit of the enterprise.

Source: Author, based on questionnaire responses.

While limited information is available regarding how performance is benchmarked since these key performance indicators (KPIs) are mostly set at the full discretion of the board (sometimes upon recommendations of the remuneration committee) and not by government – and thus vary across companies, many countries mention that performance is benchmarked against profitability relative to other companies and compared to the previous year. In many countries, performance of the CEO is also benchmarked against both corporate (SOE-level) and individual performance indicators. Financial and non-financial indicators can be both qualitative and quantitative.

In some countries, KPIs are set by government or shareholding ministers. In **New Zealand**, for state-owned enterprises and crown entities (falling under the respective legislative frameworks of the same names), performance is benchmarked against the targets set in the Statement of Corporate Intent and Statement of Performance Expectations (respectively). These are documents that comprise annual, publically accountable, key performance indicators and are approved by shareholding and responsible ministers before the start of each financial year. In **Korea** and the **Philippines**, guidance and criteria for eligibility to performance-based remuneration are set by law (Box 3.1). In **Switzerland**, while the board is responsible for setting detailed KPIs, Article 8 of the ordonnance sur la rémunération provides general guidance by stating that "bonuses are generally based on the average performance over at least two years and are increased or decreased accordingly. Both financial and qualitative criteria shall be applied as assessment criteria".

Box 3.1. Criteria and methods for evaluating the performance of executive managers of SOEs in Korea and the Philippines

Korea

According to Article 48 of the *Act on Management of Public Institutions*, the criteria and methods for the evaluation of management performance should be prescribed by the Minister of Economy and Finance through deliberation and resolution by the Steering Committee, in such a manner that the following matters should be included in the evaluation of a public corporation or quasi-governmental institution:

1. The rationality and achievement level of management goals
2. The public nature and efficiency of major projects
3. The adequacy of organisational and personnel management, including types of employment of employees
4. Soundness in financial management and budget-saving efforts, including the implementation of the mid- and long-term financial management plan established under Article 39-2
5. Results of the customer satisfaction survey conducted under Article 13 (2)
6. Operation of a rational performance-based payment system
7. Other matters related to the management of the public corporation or quasi-governmental institution.

Financial and non-financial performance targets and indicators are newly determined each year by the consultation of the Ministry of Economy and Finance, the evaluation team for the management of public corporations and quasi-governmental institutions, and SOEs subject for evaluation.

According to Article 27 of the *Enforcement Decree of the Act on the Management of Public Institutions*, the Minister of Economy and Finance shall prepare a manual for the management performance evaluation before the beginning of each fiscal year, and may, after deliberation and resolution by the Steering Committee, take follow-up measures, such as making suggestions or demands concerning personnel or budgetary actions, or deciding on the piece rate.

Philippines

Eligibility for the performance-based bonus (PBB) is anchored on both the performance of the SOE and of the individual executive manager. Certain eligibility requirements are set by *GCG M.C. No. 2019-02*, as detailed below:

Table 3.2. Eligibility criteria for performance-based compensation in the Philippine

SOE level	Individual level
At least 90% in the SOE Performance Scorecard	At least "satisfactory" ratings based on the SOE's Strategic Performance Management System (SPMS)
Satisfaction of Good Governance Conditions that are common to National Government Agencies and Specific to SOEs	Length of service: at least nine months for a full grant; at least three months but less than nine months for a pro-rated grant
Compliance to all other conditions and requirements	Compliance to all other conditions and requirements

Source: Author, based on country responses to the OECD questionnaire.

Table 3.3. Remuneration policies and practices for executive managers of SOEs across 34 jurisdictions

Country	Remuneration-setting procedures	Additional provisions
Australia	The Remuneration Tribunal allocates each principal executive offices (PEO) to a classification band, which it then publishes, the highest being Band E which allows fixed remuneration above USD 570 000, with no upper limit. The Tribunal also writes to each SOE Board Chair periodically (generally annually) to advise the Tribunal's determination of the PEO's reference rate for fixed remuneration, which is determined by the Tribunal in accordance with the PEO's Band. The Board then has discretion to set PEO fixed remuneration between 10% below and 5% above the Tribunal reference rate. Boards also have discretion to set and assess performance incentive payments, but must have regard to any guidance the Tribunal may provide.	○ ■[1]
Austria	Executive managers are appointed on fixed-term contracts of up to five years, as provided by the law governing the filling of positions (*Stellenbesetzungsgesetz BGBl. I 26/1998*). While the Federal Ministry which exercises ownership functions is responsible for the appointment of management board members of SOEs under the legal form of limited liability companies (GmbH), members of the management board of stock corporations (*Aktiengesellschaft*) are appointed by the supervisory board. Overall, SOE boards usually set remuneration levels at their own discretion, taking in consideration the company's orientation, as well as remuneration levels of comparable private companies. Overall, executive remuneration of public policy-oriented SOEs additionally includes a variable component amounting up to 20% of the annual salary, whereas it does not include pension payments or shares. By contrast, the variable components of commercially oriented SOEs vary depending on the sector of operation. Pension payments are predominantly included. The performance-related components mainly consist of a mix of short-term and long-term variable remuneration.	● ■
Belgium	For the SOEs in the Ministry of Finance's portfolio (i.e. Skeyes, NMBS/SCNB, Proximus, Bpost), the remuneration of the executive committee and the individual remuneration packages are set by the board of directors upon recommendations from the nomination and remuneration committee, and taking into account the remuneration cap on the basic remuneration for the CEO of the SOEs, which amounts to EUR 290 000 a year (gross salary). The individual remuneration packages are defined by the board according to the individual responsibilities, performance and skills of executive managers.	● ■
Brazil	All executive managers of Brazilian SOEs are appointed on fixed-term contracts. According to the *State-Owned Company Act (13.303/2016)*, the terms are limited to two years, and renewable three times. Similar to the process for determining the remuneration policy of boards, the remuneration of SOEs' executive managers is determined by the annual general meeting of the SOE. However, SOE boards participate in this process by constructing the remuneration proposal to be submitted to the Ministry of the Economy, to be further deliberated during the annual general meeting. A "People Committee" was recently established in all SOEs to advise the board on issues related to human resources management, including executive remuneration.	●[2] ■
Bulgaria	The contracts of management and supervisory board members of SOEs are concluded for a period of three to five years. However, in the case of listed SOEs, the contracts with the executive directors are open-ended and are in force until their release. Similar to the process for determining board remuneration, each ministry/holding determines the policies/rules/guidelines of the remuneration of the management and control bodies in public enterprises from its portfolio. In the case of state-owned enterprises established under Article 62 of the *Commercial Act*, the calculations themselves are carried out by each public enterprise. In the case of listed SOEs, remuneration is determined by the general meeting of shareholders in accordance with the provisions of the statute of the company and the remuneration policy.	○ ■
Chile	Executive managers are appointed on continuous contracts with terms for termination. Boards set the remuneration levels of executive managers, within the limits provided by *Circular N°15 of 2018*, which states that they must correspond to the remuneration of the first quartile of the market and cannot exceed the remuneration of the President of the Central Bank.	○ ◪
Colombia	While each SOE sets the contractual relationship with their executive managers, the MHCP has recently opted to promote the adoption of continuous contracts for SOEs operating in the electric power sector, with the rights, obligations and termination characteristics of common full time labor contracts in Colombian law (*Codigo Sustantivo del Trabajo*). In some financial institutions and other mixed economy entities and companies that carry out an industrial or commercial activity and that are owned by the state, the President of the country appoints a public official as the executive manager of the company. In this case, the company adopts the rights, obligations and termination characteristics for public servants defined by the Administrative Department of the Public Function (Departamento Administrativo de la Función Publica – DAFP) with <u>Decree 1 042 of 1978</u>, <u>Law 4 of 1992</u> and more recently <u>Decree 304 of 2020</u>.	⊙ ■

Country	Remuneration-setting procedures	Additional provisions
	The remuneration levels of executive managers are set at the discretion of the board, and sometimes ratified by the general assembly. However, if the executive manager is designated by the state according to the bylaws of the company, then the executive manager will be compensated according to the salary scale for public servants of the Administrative Department of the Public Function (Departamento Administrativo de la Función Pública – DAFP), which sets monthly remuneration caps defined in articles 1 and 49 of Decree 304 of 2020. While it is not systematic, in some cases, the SOE board sets up a committee for advising on the remuneration of executive managers and senior employees.	⊙ ◆
Costa Rica	In the majority of SOEs, the CEO is appointed on fixed-term contracts of four to six years, and the rest of the executive managers are appointed on continuous contracts with terms for termination. In only a few SOEs, both the CEO and the rest of the executives are all appointed on fixed-term contracts of four to six years. Remuneration practices for SOE executive managers are established through two different procedures, according to their orientation. For commercially oriented SOEs – including SOEs in the financial, electricity, telecommunications and postal sectors – the board has the ultimate responsibility for establishing remuneration levels of executive managers following private sector benchmarks, within the provisions set by the Law for Strengthening Public Finances. For SOEs where a remuneration committee is established, the remuneration committee is responsible for developing remuneration proposals for the board's consideration. For public policy-oriented SOEs, executive managers are subject to the public employment scheme, and applicable remuneration levels are therefore defined by the National Budgetary Authority.	
Croatia	All SOEs appoint executive managers on fixed-term contracts of up to four years, although these contracts might occasionally last six months. For all majority-owned SOEs, the salaries of CEOs and members of the management board are mainly determined according to the conditions set out in the 2009 Government "Decision on Determining Salaries and Other Remunerations of Presidents and Members of Management Boards", which sets a cap on the basic and variable components of executive managers' compensation. Although the decision is no longer in force, the provisions of the decision have however continued to apply. Overall, a remuneration policy has yet to be developed for members of both supervisory boards and management boards of state-owned enterprises, which will be the result of joint work between line ministries, MPGI and CERP, as ownership bodies.	○ ■
Czech Republic	The remuneration policy is determined by the Remuneration Principles, for which the Ministry of Finance is responsible, while their application to the relevant entities is the responsibility of the line ministries. The principles are observed in all SOEs with the exception of financial institutions which are subject to specific banking regulation (Directive 2013/36 / EU of the European Parliament and of the Council).	○
Estonia	The executive managers are typically appointed on fixed-term contracts for a maximum period of five years, subject to termination at any time. The supervisory board is responsible for setting the remuneration of the management board. While monthly remuneration is not regulated, the State Assets Act stipulates that it be kept at reasonable yet competitive level. On the other hand, annual bonuses are capped at four times the average of the monthly salary.	○ ■
Finland	Executive managers are appointed on continuous contracts with terms for termination. The board of directors decides on the managers' remuneration, which is expected to be in line with market levels. In addition, the government publishes the political guidelines on bonus levels for SOEs, which sets clear limits for the bonuses. The maximum percentage of acceptable variable remuneration varies according to company category and the categories used in this context are a) listed or major commercial companies, b) small and medium sized commercial companies, and c) special assignment companies.	● ▣
France	Executive managers are appointed on fixed-term contracts. The procedure for determining the remuneration of executive managers is similar to the one in place in private companies, as it is submitted by the board – upon recommendations of the remuneration committee – to the general meeting of the companies which approves them (or not). It is capped at EUR 450 000 per year.	● ■
Germany	Executive remuneration is set either by the board or the AGM depending on the SOE's corporate form, total number of employees, and its Charter or Articles of Association. Executive managers are appointed on fixed-term contracts for five years (and three years for the first term).	⊙ ■
Greece	The chair, vice chair and executive director of SOEs falling under the scope of Law 3429/2005 are appointed for a three-year term with the possibility of renewal for another three years. A special committee interviews the candidates and selects the most suitable for the position (according to articles 20-23 L.4735/20). Board members of SOEs which are exempted from this law are elected by the shareholders' general meeting and are appointed on fixed-term contracts according to each SOE's statute or founding law. Similar to the process applicable to boards, remuneration of executive managers is either determined by Law 4354/2015, which sets the wage grid for the public sector including SOEs, or by the AGM (for listed SOEs), in which case HCAP's candidates committee submits its recommendation to the board of HCAP.	● ■[3]

Country	Remuneration-setting procedures	Additional provisions
Hungary	Executive managers are appointed on continuous contracts with terms for termination. Boards define the remuneration policies at their own discretion, using the non-binding remuneration guideline for SOEs prepared by NVTNM according to the rules of *Act 122 of 2009 on the more efficient operation of SOEs*. The involvement of remuneration committees is at the discretion of each SOE, as they are not mandatory for SOEs (only audit committees are). While performance-related compensation is not granted to executive managers, they may receive a premium of up to 20% of their annual basic salary if a company's after-tax profit is positive. It may be higher in justified cases.	⊙ ▣
Iceland	Executive managers are usually appointed on continuous contracts with terms for termination, like in the private sector. Boards are responsible for evaluating and deciding on the remuneration of their CEOs, in line with the remuneration guidelines established by the Ministry of Finance and Economic Affairs in the state general ownership policy, which posits that the remuneration of SOE executive managers should be competitive but not market leading. Although executive managers do not receive performance-related compensation, they receive benefits (i.e. car benefits in most cases) in addition to their annual salary.	▣
Ireland	CEOs are typically hired on fixed-term contracts, while other senior executive are hired on continuous contracts. According to the Code of Practice, the contract terms of a CEO of a commercial state body is limited to a non-renewable contract of five to seven years, while CEOs of non-commercial state bodies are appointment for a term of five years, unless otherwise provided for in the body's establishing legislation.

Regarding commercial state bodies, in 2011, the government introduced revised salary ranges for new appointments to CEO posts, representing reductions of up to 25%. To date, salaries remain aligned with these ranges, and any variations have been established on a case-by-case basis as agreed with the relevant government departments and relevant ministers, and the SOE. Regarding posts in non-commercial state bodies, salaries were reduced by Financial Emergency legislation in the period 2010 to 2013. Restoration of these reductions commenced in 2017. In general, salaries remain at or below the rates that pertained prior to 2010.

Performance-related awards (PRAs) granted to CEOs of both commercial and non-commercial state bodies were suspended in 2009 in the context of the global economic downturn, and have not been reintroduced since. For executive managers below CEO level in commercial state bodies, this is a matter for the remuneration committee as appointed by the board. | ⊙ ◆ [4] |
| **Israel** | official guidelines for the remuneration of executive managers were issued in 2015, which provide that executive managers' contracts be limited to five years with the possibility of an extension of up to two years according to a board decision, to be extended by another year with the approval of the Government Companies Authority (GCA). The remuneration of the CEO is determined by virtue of a government decision, in accordance with the circular of the GCA. The salary is linked to the consumer price index or the average wages of production workers. Remuneration policies are set by the Government Companies Authority (GCA) in co-operation with the Wages and Labour Agreements Division, which are two units under the Ministry of Finance. While in practice, the board sets the remuneration levels according to the framework provided by the GCA, any deviations from the framework is based on the approval of the GCA. The board is responsible for approving promotions, and also plays a role in setting performance-based compensation and in conducting performance evaluations. | ○ ■ |
| **Japan** | Similar to the procedure in place for determining the remuneration of board members, the maximum remuneration of executive managers is approved at the Annual General Meeting based on recommendations of the Advisory Panel on Nomination and Compensation for SOEs with such committees in place (otherwise it is based on a proposal submitted by the Board). The remuneration of individual executives is determined by the board of directors within the range of the total approved amount. | ■ ● |
| **Korea** | Executive managers (or executive officials) of SOEs include the institution's head (the CEO), board of directors (executive and non-executive) and auditors (executive and non-executive). They are in a contractual relationship with the SOE boards, the Committee for Recommendation of Executive Officers, the line ministry, and the Ministry of Economy and Finance. They are appointed on fixed-term contracts, the institution head (the CEO)'s term being three years, and the directors and auditors being two years. An executive officer of a public corporation and quasi-governmental institution may be consecutively appointed for one-year terms. All executive managers of every public institution in Korea are subject to the same, basic contractual standards under the *Act on the Management of Public Institutions*, so there is no difference across SOEs.

According to *Article 33 of the Act on the Management of Public Institutions* and *Article 5 of the attached Guidelines for Remuneration for Executive Officers of Public Corporations and Quasi-governmental institutions*, the guidelines for remuneration of executive officers of a public corporation or quasi-governmental institution shall be determined by the board of directors in accordance with the guidelines for remuneration determined by the Minister of Strategy and Finance through the deliberation and resolution by the Steering Committee. Further, according to Article 4 of the *Guidelines*, the basic annual salary of the head of the corporation shall be determined annually in connection with the annual salary of the vice | ■ ● |

Country	Remuneration-setting procedures	Additional provisions
	minister among public officials in political service. The annual salary of vice ministers are determined each year by the Ministry of Personnel Management (MPM) at the state council, based on the *Public Officials Remuneration Regulations* and *Regulations on Allowances for Public Officials*. For reference, as of 2021, the Vice Minister's annual salary was set at roughly 132 million won. In addition, the basic annual salary of a standing auditor and a standing director shall be equal to 80% of the basic annual salary of the CEO. This cap applies to both the basic annual salary and management performance bonuses. While board committees can be involved in determining the remuneration levels of executive managers, this depends on whether they are set up, as they are not mandatory in SOEs.	
Latvia	Members of the management board in SOEs are appointed for a fixed five-year term, renewable once upon the decision of the ownership entity or supervisory board. In cases where it is not possible to complete the nomination procedure of the management board member within a term that would ensure the operational capacity of the SOE, a member of the management board may be appointed on a temporary basis (not exceeding one year). The boards set the remuneration of executive managers, within the limits provided by law as well as the central ownership agency's guidelines explaining the application of remuneration principles in practice. In particular, the remuneration of the CEO of a small SOE may not exceed five times the average statistical salary of the previous year, while the CEO of a medium-sized SOE may not exceed it by eight times, and of a large SOE, by 10 times. The remuneration levels of the members of the executive boards are capped by 90% of the remuneration of the CEO. Overall, the ownership entity (or supervisory board) should ensure that increases in monthly remuneration amounts do not exceed 25% of the amount reported during the previous year.	⊙[5] ■
Lithuania	CEOs of SOEs are hired for a five-year term, renewable once, provided that all operational objectives of the SOEs are achieved. The policy of the remuneration of senior executives of SOEs is regulated by *Resolution No 1.341 of the Government of the Republic of Lithuania of 23 August 2002*. The Remuneration Resolution regulates only the remuneration of CEOs and deputy directors of statutory enterprises (including 17 SOEs). For state-owned limited liability companies (including 32 SOEs), the provisions of the *Remuneration Resolution* are only recommended in principle, but widely followed in practice. For statutory SOEs, the actual salary of executive managers is set by the ownership entity (usually the line ministry), within the range set by law. Line ministries also decide on the variable remuneration component of executive managers, respecting the established limits set by law. Boards of limited liability SOEs have much more flexibility to set the remuneration amounts for the executives, as the ownership entity can decide not to comply with the provisions of the Remuneration Resolution. Although remuneration committees can play a role in recommending remuneration policies as well as in monitoring their implementation, they are not widely established in SOEs (only three boards have set up such committees).	⊙[6] ■
Mexico	Executive managers of PEMEX are hired on fixed-term contracts, while for CFE, executive managers are public servants appointed on continuous contracts. In the case of PEMEX, the Human Resources and Remuneration Committee is responsible for proposing to the board of directors the remuneration mechanism for the CEO and the executives standing three hierarchical levels below him/her. The CEO remuneration is capped at the amount equivalent to the remuneration of a Secretary of State (MXN 158 270 [Mexican Pesos], monthly). In the case of CFE, according to its statutory law (*CFE Law*), the Human Resources and Remuneration Committee proposes to the board of directors the remuneration mechanism for the CEO and executive managers three hierarchical levels below him/her, within the limits provided by the approved budget and without exceeding the budget ceiling for Chapter 1 000 "Personal Services" of the Classifier by Object of Expenditure.	●◆[7]
Netherlands	Executive managers of all SOEs are appointed on fixed-term contracts. According to the Government's SOE board remuneration policy, the maximum remuneration amount for executive managers of individual SOEs is decided by the general meeting of shareholders, using as a reference the Top Income Standard Law (*de Wet Normering Topinkomens*) for public policy-oriented SOEs, and the median of a private peer group of similar companies for commercially oriented SOEs. Once the limits have been set, the supervisory board decides on the actual remuneration levels of the members of the executive board.	■
New Zealand	Chief executives are usually appointed by boards on continuous employment contracts, although this is at the discretion of boards. For commercial SOEs, CEO remuneration is determined by each company's board, which are generally expected to use benchmarks of similar sized companies operating in similar industries. For public policy-oriented companies, the State Services Commissioner provides recommendations to the boards of statutory crown entities on chief executive remuneration. However, as the employer of chief executives, boards are ultimately responsible for agreeing the terms and conditions with their chief executives. The Public Service Commission publishes Public Sector Senior	●⊡

Country	Remuneration-setting procedures	Additional provisions
	Pay in a compiled report from time to time, which can also be used as a benchmarking tool for commercial SOEs. Overall, the more profit-oriented the company, the more likely the board will use private sector benchmarks.	● ▣
Norway	Executive managers are appointed on continuous contracts with terms for termination. The Norwegian state's guidelines for remuneration of senior executives in companies with state ownership, established by the Ministry of Trade, Industry and Fisheries, outline expectations for remuneration of the executive management in SOEs. The board is required to produce guidelines for executive remuneration, as mandated by law for listed public limited liability companies, and by the companies' articles of association for all other non-small SOEs. The guidelines shall be approved by the general meeting and will be binding on the board's actual implementation of the remuneration policy. While the board is responsible for setting the remuneration of the CEO (within the board's guidelines), the CEO is responsible for setting the remuneration of the rest of the executive managers (within the board's guidelines). Many SOE boards have compensation committees which provide recommendations to the board regarding the remuneration levels of executive managers. There are no remuneration caps or limits regarding fixed compensation levels, although the state expects the remuneration to be competitive but not market leading, and that the boards take moderation into account when setting the remuneration. However, boards should respect limits related to pensions, severance pay (amounting to six months' salary plus the salary in the resignation period), and performance-based pay.	
Philippines	The CEO or the highest-ranking officer provided in the charters of the SOEs shall be elected annually by the members of the board from among its ranks. The CEO shall be subject to the disciplinary powers of the board and may be removed by the board for cause. Notably, the term of office of a CEO appointed to the board is for one year, unless sooner removed for cause, in which case he/she shall continue to hold office until the successor is appointed. The remuneration of executive managers is set by the compensation and position classification system for SOEs, following the principles set under Section 9 of R.A. No. 10149. As such, the state ownership agency (GCG) establishes and/or recommends to the Office of the President of the Philippines, as may be required or needed, the remuneration policies covering SOEs. Such policies may be co-ordinated with key government agencies such as the Department of Budget and Management, and the Department of Finance. Overall, the remuneration levels of executive managers of SOEs are either fixed by law or approved by the President of the Philippines. In particular, for SOEs that follow the Salary Standardization Law (SSL), their compensation is provided by E.O. No. 36, s. 2017 and its implementing rules and regulations (IRR) under GCG M.C. No. 2017-03. On the other hand, for SOEs that are applying a compensation framework that is different from the SSL, their remuneration must bear the necessary approval from the Office of the President of the Philippines, as provided under Joint Resolution (J.R.) No. 4 s. 2009, Section 5 of Presidential Decree (P.D.) No. 1597, s. 1978, Section 9 of E.O. No. 7, s. 2010 and R.A. No. 10149.	○ ■
Portugal	According to Article 13 of Decree-Law No. 71/2007 of 27 March, executive managers are designated by means of appointment or election. If the designation is made by appointment, it is carried out by a Council of Ministers Resolution published in the Official Gazette. Executive managers' positions are held, as a rule, for a three-year period that shall not be renewed more than three times. Similar to the remuneration of board members, the government also establishes the remuneration policies for executive managers. These are set according to Resolution of the Council of Ministers No. 16/2012 of 14 February 2012, which classifies SOEs into three groups (A, B and C) based on the application of the following indicators: i) contribution of the public financial effort to the operating result; ii) number of employees; iii) net assets; iv) turnover. Overall, the monthly compensation of executive manager cannot exceed the Prime Minister's compensation.	○ ■
Slovak Republic	In most of the SOEs, CEOs conclude the mandate contract according to the Slovak Commercial Code, while the CFOs, COOs and other executive managers work under terms of the Slovak Labour Code. The tenure of a CEO is usually set to five years and may be terminated by her/his resignation or completion of the five-year term. The tenure of the other executive managers depends on the conditions in their labour contracts, which are mostly concluded for an indefinite period of time with terms for termination. The remuneration of executive managers is decided at the AGM based on a proposal submitted by the supervisory board, taking into account the provisions of relevant rules and regulations for wholly owned SOEs and for state enterprises. For 100%-owned SOEs, the Resolution of the Slovak Government No. 159/2011 provides that the remuneration of the members of the management board consist of three components: i) a fixed component set as a 1.5-2 multiple of the average nominal wage, based on data provided by the Statistical Office of the Slovak Republic; ii) a component of economic nature reflecting the size of the SOE and its role within the economy (e.g. return on investment, etc.); and iii) a variable component capped at 50% of the amount of the first two components. For state enterprises, according to the Act No. 111/1990 Coll. on State Enterprise, the monthly salary of the	○ ◆

Country	Remuneration-setting procedures	Additional provisions
	CEO of a state enterprise cannot exceed eight times the average wage in the national economy of the previous year, and the annual remuneration (share on profit/royalties) cannot exceed 10% of the disposal profit of the enterprise.	● ▣
Sweden	Executive managers are usually appointed on continuous contracts with terms for termination. According to the State Ownership Policy and principles for state-owned enterprises, the total remuneration paid to senior officers is to be competitive, but not market leading. The board sets the remuneration level of the CEO at its full discretion, based on a proposal formulated by the remuneration committee following a benchmarking exercise. The board also has full discretion to set the remuneration levels of the other members of the management board, although it is based on a proposal submitted by the CEO. Likewise, the board evaluates the CEO performance, and the CEO evaluate the performance of members of the management board, which are used to determine the actual salary change. Executive managers do not receive performance-related compensation. However, in addition to their fixed, cash-based salary, they receive severance pay, pension benefits and other benefits (such as a company car).	
Switzerland	The contractual relationship of executive managers with the company is in most cases an employment contract based on the Swiss Code of Obligations. Therefore, both fixed-term contracts as well as continuous contracts with terms for termination are possible. Similar to the process for determining board remuneration, executive remuneration is determined by the company based on relevant rules and regulations. For companies limited by shares, the annual general meeting has the power to determine annually i) a ceiling for the total amount of the fees of the board members and its chair (separately) and ii) to set an upper limit for the total amount of the remuneration of the executive board.	◆ ●
Turkey	According to Decree Law No. 233, the members of the SOE board of directors are appointed by the President to serve for three years. It should be noted that the remuneration is the same for executive and non-executive members, as the upper remuneration limit for each SOE is determined by presidential decision, which was drafted by the Ministry of Treasury and Finance, taking into consideration inputs from the relevant Ministries and the Presidency. While the remuneration of specific SOEs can be up to 45% higher than in other SOEs, the number of these "privileged" SOEs is small. Overall, two monthly benefits are granted to executive managers annually – albeit not related to performance – in addition to the fixed fees received over 12 months.	○ ▣
United Kingdom	Executive managers are usually appointed on open-ended contracts. Remuneration for SOEs is set in the same way that private companies set their remuneration. The process is led by the Remuneration Committee, which will often engage external remuneration consultants to help devise packages and benchmark against comparators. Based on the Remuneration Committee's recommendation, the board sets remuneration levels at its own discretion, within the broad rules established by government regarding spending public money as set out in Managing Public Money and the Guidance for the Approval of Senior Pay. These policies are set by HM Treasury and apply across all government departments, and provide that all remuneration must be cash-based and that few allowances/benefits are allowed. For the CEO or CFO (and in some cases other employees), all packages above GBP 150k must be approved by ministers.	● ▣

Notes: Data unavailable for **Peru** and **Spain**. On role of board committees in setting remuneration levels: ● = yes; ○ = no; ⊙ = ad-hoc basis. On contractual relationships of executive managers: ■ = fixed-term contracts; ▣ = open-ended contracts; ◆ = both possible.

[1] In **Australia**, although board committees do not play a role, boards are consulted on an annual basis.

[2] In **Brazil**, a "People Committee" was recently established in all SOEs to advise the board on human resources management issues, including executive remuneration.

[3] In **Greece**, the remuneration committee plays a role in listed SOEs only.

[4] In **Ireland**, the remuneration committee plays a role with regard to the remuneration of executive managers below CEO level in commercial state bodies only. In addition, while CEOs are hired on fixed-term contracts, other executive managers are usually hired on continuous contracts with terms for termination.

[5] In **Latvia**, the role of the remuneration committee is mandatory for listed SOEs, but is not widespread practice for other SOEs.

[6] In **Lithuania**, only three SOE boards have a remuneration committee.

[7] In **Mexico**, fixed-term for PEMEC, open-ended for civil servants as executive manager (CFE).

Source: Author, based on questionnaire responses and desk research.

3.4. Transparency and disclosure practices

On the issue of transparency and disclosure, the *SOE Guidelines* observe that "[i]t is important that SOEs ensure high levels of transparency regarding the remuneration of board members and key executives. Failure to provide adequate information to the public could result in negative perceptions and fuel risks of a backlash against the ownership entity and individual SOEs. Information should relate to actual remuneration levels and the policies that underpin them" (annotations to Chapter VI, Point A). It indicates that it is considered in the interest of ownership entities to opt for maximum transparency, even at the risk of spurring public anger by disclosing pay levels that may be considered as excessive.

3.4.1. Disclosure practices by SOEs

In all but two countries (**Turkey** and **Colombia**)[1], SOEs are required to disclose information on the remuneration levels of executive managers to the general public. In many countries, SOEs also disclose the remuneration policy applicable to executive managers, including some details of the bonus schemes and key performance indicators underpinning the calculation of the variable remuneration amount (e.g. **Australia**, **Belgium**, **United Kingdom**). In **Latvia**, while SOEs were previously only required to publish the principles of their remuneration policy, since January 2020, majority-owned SOEs are required to disclose remuneration levels of individual executive managers.

In some countries, different requirements apply depending on the legal form, share of state ownership, orientation and size of the company. For instance, in the **Czech Republic**, granular information on the remuneration of each executive manager is required to be disclosed by listed SOEs only, while non-listed SOEs are only required to disclose general information in their annual reports. In **Israel**, only listed and "non-profit" companies are required to disclose this information. In the **Netherlands**, while the Dutch Corporate Governance Code is only mandatory for listed companies, and prescribes that the remuneration of executive managers be published on the SOE's websites, all SOEs comply. In **Croatia**, similar to provisions applicable to supervisory boards, listed SOEs are required to disclose the remuneration of individual executive managers and of the entire management board, in addition to the remuneration policy. Unlisted SOEs have not such obligation.

In **New Zealand**, while there are no legally binding disclosure requirements for SOEs, since 2019, the government expects commercially oriented SOEs to disclose the remuneration of the CEO and CFO, in an effort to align SOE practices with the provisions applicable to listed companies. In addition, according to Section 211 (1)(g) of the *Companies Act 1993*, all SOEs and listed companies are legally required to publicly disclose the number of employees which are paid more than NZD 100 000 (New Zealand dollars). Likewise, In the **United Kingdom**, while SOEs are required to disclose information on executives in their annual report, for those not classified as "public corporations" there is also a requirement to disclose the base remuneration of all employees earning a base salary of more than GBP 150k.

In **Ireland**, the *Code of Practice for the Governance of State Bodies* sets out that commercial state bodies, in addition to disclosing the aggregate pay bill and total number of employees, should publish details on the number of employees whose total employee benefits (excluding employer pension costs) for the reporting period fell within each band of EUR 25 000 from EUR 50 000 upwards and an overall figure for total employer pension contributions in their annual report and/or financial statements.

This information is most often required to be disclosed by SOEs in their annual reports or on their websites, but in some countries, a separate remuneration report is required. For instance, in **Belgium**, the remuneration committee is required by law to produce a report on the remuneration of the members of the executive committee, which is included in the annual report. In **Sweden**, SOEs have to prepare a remuneration report, like listed limited liability companies as per the *Companies Act* and *Annual Accounts*

Act, disclosing the remuneration of executive managers and accounting how the government's principles for remuneration and other terms of employment have been applied. A similar requirement to prepare a remuneration report has been imposed on non-small SOEs in **Norway** effective from 2023. Further, according to the *Accounting Act*, all companies that are not small shall report the aggregate salary provided to the CEO.

While SOEs are only required to disclose the remuneration of the CEO in some countries (**Iceland**, **Lithuania**), in other countries, disclosure is divided between CEO remuneration and remuneration of the rest of the management team on an aggregate basis (**Australia**, **Belgium**, **Finland**). In some countries, some SOEs also disclose disaggregated information on the fixed and variable remuneration components, and the weight of each part in the overall pay packages of the CEO and other executive managers (**Estonia**, **Belgium**).

Box 3.2. Example of granular disclosure on executive remuneration by a Belgium SOE (Proximus)

In its integrated annual report, Proximus provides a general overview of the remuneration allocated to the members of the Executive Committee over the last five years, with disaggregated information on each remuneration component, split between pay packages of the CEO and the other members of the Executive Committee.

Table 3.4. Remuneration overview of the CEO

CEO	2016	2017	2018	2019	2020
Fixed remuneration	EUR 505.005	EUR 515.108	EUR 522.810	EUR 429.498	EUR 507.492
Short-term variable remuneration	EUR 178.875	EUR 227.195	EUR 225.295	EUR 215.661	EUR 458.833
Long-term variable remuneration	EUR 0	EUR 0	EUR 0	EUR 0	EUR 18.833
Group insurance premiums	EUR 169.666	EUR 181.243	EUR 180.003	EUR 157.433	EUR 78.550
Other benefits	EUR 12.463	EUR 13.357	EUR 12.438	EUR 17.619	EUR 55.083
Subtotal (excl. employer's social contributions)	EUR 866.009	EUR 936.903	EUR 940.546	EUR 820.211	EUR 1.118.791
Termination benefits	EUR 0	EUR 0	EUR 0	EUR 0	EUR 0
Total (excl. employer's social contributions)	EUR 866.009	EUR 936.903	EUR 940.546	EUR 820.211	EUR 1.118.791

Source: Proximus Group (2020), Integrated Annual Report 2020, https://www.proximus.com/annualreport2020.html.

Table 3.5. Remuneration overview of the other members of the Executive Committee

Other members of the Executive Committee	2016	2017	2018	2019	2020
Fixed remuneration	EUR 2.497.345	EUR 2.253.540	EUR 2.466.946	EUR 2.632.038	EUR 2.166.045
Short-term variable remuneration	EUR 1.583.327	EUR 1.105.537	EUR 1.110.745	EUR 1.070.733	EUR 1.807.390
Long-term variable remuneration	EUR 982.000	EUR 1.005.000	EUR 1.025.000	EUR 1.055.000	EUR 916.375
Group insurance premiums	EUR 919.496	EUR 516.193	EUR 494.319	EUR 529.369	EUR 468.275
Other benefits	EUR 107.605	EUR 108.433	EUR 124.172	EUR 145.588	EUR 135.648
Subtotal (excl. employer's social contributions)	EUR 6.098.773	EUR 4.988.703	EUR 5.221.182	EUR 5.432.728	EUR 5.493.733
Termination benefits	EUR 0	EUR 0	EUR 0	EUR 0	EUR 0
Total (excl. employer's social contributions)	EUR 6.089.773	EUR 4.988.703	EUR 5.221.182	EUR 5.432.728	EUR 5.493.733

Source: Proximus Group (2020), Integrated Annual Report 2020, https://www.proximus.com/annualreport2020.html.

Proximus also discloses the weight of each remuneration component in the overall pay packages of the CEO and rest of the executive committee in a given year.

Figure 3.5. Relative importance of the various components of the remuneration effectively allocated in 2020 before employer's social contribution

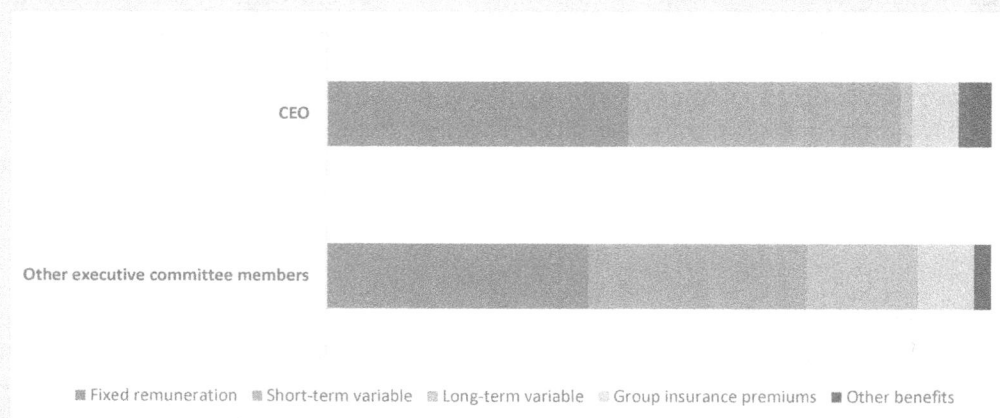

Source: Proximus Group (2020), Integrated Annual Report 2020, https://www.proximus.com/annualreport2020.html.

In **Colombia**, while SOEs are not required to disclose information on the remuneration levels or policy, SOEs are encouraged by the ownership entity to disclose this information, especially for companies where the President appoints a public official as executive manager. In the **Slovak Republic**, only joint stock companies and state enterprises are required to disclose remuneration information on an aggregate basis. While the law provides for levels to be disclosed upon request, it is reported that in practice, SOEs rarely comply.

3.4.2. Disclosure practices by the state or ownership entity

In almost half of the surveyed countries with available information (15 out of 33), the state or ownership entity does not disclose information on the remuneration of executive managers, mainly because SOEs are already required to do so in their annual reports or on their websites (e.g. **Austria**, **Belgium**, **Chile**, **Estonia**, **Finland**, **Japan**, **New Zealand**), or because remuneration caps are set by law which is itself publicly available (e.g. **Turkey**). This may also be because in these countries, setting the remuneration of executive managers is the responsibility of the board and not the state.

In some of these countries, while executive remuneration is not disclosed on a systematic basis, SOEs are legally required to disclose the monthly remuneration of public officials appointed by the government as executive managers in SOEs (**Colombia**, **Latvia**). In **Costa Rica**, similar to boards, while information on remuneration is not actively disclosed by the ownership entity, the Presidential Advisory Unit on State Ownership does disclose whether specific SOEs are complying with their responsibility to publish the required board and management remuneration information, as part of the analysis included in the annual Aggregate Report on SOEs.

Out of the 16 countries where the government discloses granular information on remuneration of executive managers, in some instances this is mainly done through a central government portal aggregating all SOE websites, making this information easily accessible to the public (**Australia**, **Korea**, **Portugal**). In **France**, the **Netherlands**, **Norway** and **Switzerland**, information on executive remuneration is disclosed in the government or ownership entity's annual report on SOEs, or by the Commission on Audit in the

Philippines. In the **United Kingdom**, the state collates and discloses the salary of all employees who earn more than GBP 150k except those employed by 'public corporations'.

In some countries, disclosure is limited to the remuneration of the CEO only (**Iceland**, **Lithuania**, **Norway**), or to the remuneration of executive managers of large SOEs only (**Bulgaria**). In **Lithuania**, since 2018 the Governance Co-ordination Centre publishes detailed analysis on CEO remuneration, both disclosing the total amount and composition of the remuneration for each SOE in its portfolio.

Figure 3.6. Disclosure of remuneration levels of executive managers by the government or ownership entity

Does the state or ownership entity disclose remuneration levels of executive managers?

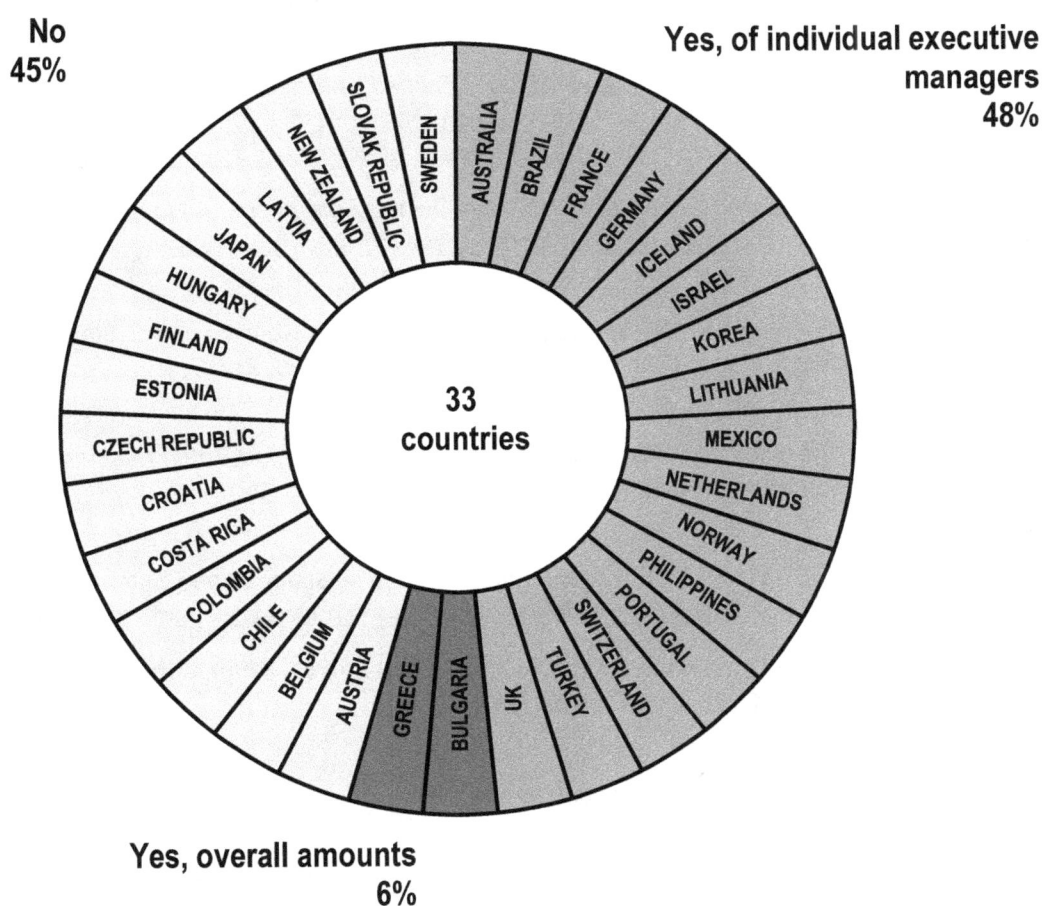

Note: Data unavailable for Ireland, Peru and Spain.
Source: Author, based on an analysis of questionnaire responses and desk research.

References

European Commission (2016), *State-Owned Enterprises in the EU: Lessons Learnt and Ways Forward in a Post-Crisis Context*, https://ec.europa.eu/info/publications/economy-finance/state-owned-enterprises-eu-lessons-learnt-and-ways-forward-post-crisis-context_en. [3]

IBP (2014), *Transparency of State-Owned Enterprises in South Korea*, https://www.internationalbudget.org/wp-content/uploads/Hidden-Corners-South-Korea.pdf. [11]

IDB (2016), *State-owned enterprise management: advantages of centralized models*, https://publications.iadb.org/publications/english/document/State-owned-Enterprise-Management-Advantages-of-Centralized-Models.pdf. [4]

Keppeler, F. and U. Papenfuß (2021), *Understanding vertical pay dispersion in the public sectir: the role of publicness for manager-to-worker pay ratios and interdisciplinary agenda for future research*, Public Management Review, https://doi.org/10.1080/14719037.2021.1942531. [5]

OECD (2022), *Monitoring the Performance of State-Owned Enterprises: Good Practice Guide for Annual Aggregate Reporting*, https://www.oecd.org/corporate/ca/Monitoring-performance-state-owned-enterprises-good-practice-guide-annual-aggregate-reporting-2022.pdf. [8]

OECD (2021), *Ownership and Governance of State-Owned Enterprises: A Compendium of National Practices*, https://www.oecd.org/corporate/ownership-and-governance-of-state-owned-enterprises-a-compendium-of-national-practices.htm. [7]

OECD (2020), *Implementing the OECD Guidelines on Corporate Governance of State-Owned Enterprises: Review of Recent Developments*, OECD Publishing, Paris, https://doi.org/10.1787/4caa0c3b-en. [12]

OECD (2020), *Transparency and Disclosure Practices of State-Owned Enterprises and their Owners*, OECD Publishing, Paris, http://www.oecd.org/corporate/transparency-disclosure-practices-soes. [9]

OECD (2015), *OECD Guidelines on Corporate Governance of State-Owned Enterprises*, https://www.oecd.org/corporate/guidelines-corporate-governance-soes.htm. [10]

OECD (2011), *Corporate Governance of State-Owned Enterprises: Change and Reform in OECD Countries since 2005*, OECD Publishing, Paris, https://doi.org/10.1787/9789264119529-en. [6]

Proximus Group (2020), *Integrated Annual Report 2020*, https://www.proximus.com/annualreport2020.html. [2]

Swedish Government (2021), *Annual report for state-owned enterprises 2020*, https://www.government.se/4a8002/contentassets/cfc739c587744fefa6e117e0f20ae788/annual-report-for-state-owned-enterprises-2020-complete.pdf. [1]

Notes

[1] In **Norway**, it is worth noting that since 2022, most SOE boards are required to prepare a remuneration policy to be approved by the general meeting, and the remuneration of the CEO and other executive managers must be set within such policy. The remuneration policy will not include limits for the overall remuneration levels.

[2] See for instance: 16.438 Entreprises fédérales et entreprises liées à la Confédération. Pour des rétributions appropriées et pour la fin des salaires excessifs ; 16.3377 Un plafond des salaires à 500000 francs.

[1] The absence of such requirements in **Turkey** can be explained by the fact that this information is already publicly available as the limits are set by law. Likewise, in **Colombia**, when public officials serve as executives their remunerations are publicly disclosed.

Annex A. SOE classification according to orientation and size

Criteria according to which state-owned enterprises (SOEs) are considered to be commercially oriented or public policy-oriented

In **Bulgaria**, **Chile**, **France**, **Greece**, the **Netherlands**, **Peru** and **Sweden**, all SOEs are classified as commercially oriented (i.e. they operate in open market competition, and must be profitable and efficient), regardless of the nature of their objectives. However, in **Greece**, SOEs which may serve a public policy are funded in part or in whole from the state budget. Information is not available for **Australia**, **Austria**, the **Slovak Republic** and **Spain**.

In **Brazil**, SOEs are classified as "dependent" and "non-dependent". While "dependent SOEs" are those that receive funds from the controlling shareholder to be spent in operational expenditure or overhead expenditures, "non-dependent SOEs" can only receive funds from the controlling shareholder to capital expenditures. For the purpose of this report, the latter are considered as 'commercial'.

In **Colombia**, CONPES 3851 of 2015 and CONPES 3927 of 2018 set out the criteria classifying SOEs according to their orientation.

- A first group includes companies that develop public policy objectives, and through which the state seeks to correct market or government failures, or participate in strategic sectors. For the companies belonging to this group, the state must have a majority participation.
- A second group includes companies that create profitability and are a source of tax revenue to the state. In that regard, these companies should have a high level of returns and contribution to the capital income of the General Budget of the Nation (PGN). These companies can operate in any sector of the economy and may be maintained in the long-term portfolio of the Nation.

In **Costa Rica**, SOEs are generally considered policy-oriented, and are considered "commercial" when, in addition to their public service mandates, they carry out their operations in open market competition. As such, commercial SOEs include the Bank of Costa Rica (BCR) and five of its subsidiaries, National Bank of Costa Rica (BNCR) and its four subsidiaries, National Insurance Company (INS) and three of its subsidiaries, Costa Rican Institute of Electricity and two of its subsidiaries, Costa Rican Mail Service S.A., National Cultural Radio and Television System (SINART), Atlantic Economic Development and Port Administration Board (JAPDEVA) and Costa Rican Institute of Ports of the Pacific Ocean (INCOP).

In the **Czech Republic**, SOEs are divided between companies (defined by *Act No. 90/2012 Coll., On Companies and Co-operatives*) and state enterprises (defined by *Act No. 77/1997 Coll., On State Enterprise*). In particular, Article 2 of the *Act on State Enterprise* defines state enterprises as fulfilling tasks of important strategic, economic, security or other state interest.

In **Estonia**, each line ministry defines whether SOEs are policy-oriented (i.e. "strategic") or commercially oriented for the companies in their portfolio. The state's 2020 consolidated annual report on SOEs summarises each SOE's orientation as of 2020 (on pp.51-52). Of note, the four SOEs in the Ministry of Finance's portfolio (operating in the energy, gambling, real estate and broadcasting sector) are each defined as both policy and commercially oriented.

In **Finland**, state ownership is based on strategic interests, financial interests or the need to fulfil a specific mission using the legal form of a limited liability company. Strategic interests may relate to national defence, the maintenance of emergency stocks of critical supplies or infrastructure, or the obligation to provide needed basic services. Special assignment companies serve a specific state-defined purpose, carrying out duties that are best organised in corporate form. The company-specific interests underlying state holdings shape the objectives for state ownership established for individual companies. Additionally, state-owned investment companies can promote domestic ownership, innovation and climate investments.

In **Ireland**, according to the Code of Practice for the Governance of State Bodies, there are three types of State bodies: commercial State bodies, non-commercial State bodies and regulatory bodies. Commercial bodies are involved in commercial activities while non-commercial bodies have regulatory, developmental, service delivery or advisory roles. State bodies generally have governing legislation which provides for, inter alia, the appointment (by the relevant Minister) of the board and the chairperson.

In **Israel**, SOEs are defined as commercially oriented, unless the government has set public policy objectives (often through stipulation in the corporate bylaws) or the SOE has been established as a non-profit company.

In **Korea**, SOEs are classified as "public institutions" and may take the form of public corporations, quasi-governmental institutions, and non-classified public institutions based on the number of personnel, self-generating revenue, and the amount of total revenue.

Public corporations are divided into market-type public corporations (public corporations whose asset size equals or exceeds two trillion won and whose self-generating revenue out of total revenue equals or exceeds 85%), and quasi-market type public corporations (public corporations other than market-type public corporations). Both market-type and quasi-market type corporations include listed SOEs, and contain the characteristics of both commercial pursuit and public policy enforcement.

Quasi-governmental institutions are divided into fund-management-type quasi-governmental institutions (quasi-governmental institutions to which the management of a fund is assigned or commissioned pursuant to the *National Finance Act*), and commissioned-service-type quasi-governmental institutions (quasi-governmental institutions other than fund-management-type quasi-governmental institutions). Public institutions not classified into either public corporations or quasi-governmental institutions are classified as non-classified public institutions.

Overall, quasi-governmental institutions were established more for the purpose of implementing public policies rather than commercial pursuit. However, some quasi-governmental institutions and non-classified public institutions, such as financial institutions, are regarded as pursuing both public policy objectives and commercial activities.

In **Latvia**, SOEs which are highly dependent on the state budget are classified as dependent non-commercial SOEs, while SOEs which are not dependent on state subsidies or other grants are considered commercial SOEs.

In **Lithuania**, SOEs can be grouped into three categories: those which provide only public policy-oriented functions (so called "special obligations"), those which provide only commercially oriented functions, and those which provide both types of functions. The criteria distinguishing public-oriented functions from commercial ones are the following:

- The obligation to provide functions is set in the law or in the government resolution.
- The financing mechanism allows to compensate only incurred expenses or due to regulation provisions, profit, in line with market conditions, is not possible.
- The function is of a public administration nature.

However, the remuneration policy of CEOs and board members of both commercially oriented and policy-oriented SOEs is not based on the type of functions performed, as the level of remuneration is mainly based on the size of SOEs and the complexity of their activities.

In **Mexico**, a decentralised ownership model exists as each line ministry oversees the SOEs in its portfolio. Overall, SOEs are classified into four categories: (i) Decentralised Agencies; (ii) Majority State-Owned Enterprises (*parastatal enterprises*) (iii) Public Trust Funds and (iv) State Productive Companies. The two SOEs considered in this report – *Comisión Federal de Electricidad* (CFE) and *Petróleos Mexicanos* (PEMEX) – are both classified as State Productive Companies, and are considered as commercial.

In **New Zealand**, the objectives of SOEs are determined by specific legislative frameworks. Profit-oriented state-owned commercial companies – locally referred to as SOEs – are governed by the *State Owned Enterprises Act 1986*. Mixed-objective state-owned commercial companies are governed by a range of legislation, predominantly the *Crown Entities Act 2004* and the *Public Finance Act 1989* (Schedule 4a companies). These companies generally have a mix of policy-oriented and commercially oriented objectives. Other forms of profit-oriented, partially owned SOEs include partially listed SOEs, and sovereign wealth funds and independent pension funds.

In **Norway**, SOEs are assigned to three categories. The companies that primarily operate in competition with others are normally placed in Categories 1 and 2 (commercially oriented), while the companies that do not primarily operate in competition with others are normally placed in Category 3 (public policy-oriented). The Norwegian state's goal as an owner for companies that are placed in Categories 1 and 2 is the highest possible return over time, while the state's goal as an owner for companies that are placed in Category 3 is to achieve the most efficient possible attainment of public policy goals.

In the **Philippines**, SOEs – locally referred to as government-owned or controlled corporations (GOCCs) – are not classified according to their orientation. Alternatively, the remuneration of SOE governing boards is based on a classification scheme anchored on their assets and revenues.

In **Switzerland**, commercially oriented SOEs carry out activities of economic nature – including offering goods and services under market conditions, while public policy-oriented SOEs either provide services for which competition is not possible or only to a limited extent due to market failure, or fulfil tasks regarding the economic and safety supervision.

In **Turkey**, SOEs subject to *Decree Law no.233* are locally referred to as Public Economic Enterprises (PEE). State Economic Enterprises (SEE) are Public Economic Enterprises which are majority-owned by the state, and are established to operate in open market competition. Public Economic Institutions (PEI) are Public Economic Enterprises which are majority-owned by the state, and are established to offer monopoly goods and services. Of note, this classification has no impact on board remuneration.

In the **United Kingdom**, many commercially oriented SOEs are classified as 'public corporations' by the independent Office of National Statistics, in line with international statistical standards and drawing on the European System of Accounts (ESA) 2010 and the Manual of Government Deficit and Debt, which stipulates that non-financial Public Corporations must derive more than 50% of their production cost from the sale of goods or services at economically significant prices. Overall, commercially oriented SOEs may deliver public policy objectives in addition to their commercial activities.

Criteria/threshold according to which state-owned enterprises (SOEs) are considered as "large", "medium-sized", and "small"

Information is unavailable for **Australia**, **Austria**, **Belgium**, **France**, **Germany** and **Mexico**.

In **Brazil**, the SOE size is based on their gross revenue. Large companies are those with an annual gross revenue greater than BRL 90 millions (Brazilian Real) (approximately USD 17.4 million per year). On the other hand, if the annual gross revenue is less than BRL 90 million/year, the company is considered to be small.

In **Bulgaria**, according to Article 4 of the *Public Enterprises Act*, SOEs are divided into four categories: 'micro', 'small', 'medium' and 'large', based on the criteria set out in Chapter 2, section I and section II of the *Accountancy Act*. In particular:

- Micro-enterprises should not exceed at least two of the following criteria:
  - book value of the assets equal to BGN 700 000 (Bulgarian Lev)
  - net sales revenue equal to BGN 1 400 000
  - average number of employees for the reporting period equal to 10.
- Small enterprises should not exceed at least two of the following criteria:
  - book value of the assets equal to BGN 8 000 000
  - net sales revenue equal to BGN 16 000 000
  - average number of employees for the reporting period equal to 50.
- Medium-sized enterprises should not exceed at least two of the following criteria:
  - book value of the assets equal to BG 38 000 000
  - net sales revenue equal to BGN 76 000 000
  - average number of employees for the reporting period equal to 250.
- Large enterprises should exceed at least two of the following criteria:
  - book value of the assets equal to BGN 38 000 000
  - net sales revenue equal to BGN 76 000 000
  - average number of employees for the reporting period equal to 250.

Board and executive remuneration is calculated using indicators and criteria for establishing a total score, and as set out in Annex 2 of the *Implementing Rules of the Law on Public Enterprises*.

Figure A.1. Indicators and criteria for establishing the total score in public enterprises in Bulgaria

Item No.	Indicators		Criteria		Score unit
1	2		3		4
1.	Value of the assets	1.1.	up to BGN 500 thousand		2,0
		1.2.	over BGN 500 thousand and up to BGN 1500 thousand		2,5
		1.3.	over BGN 1500 thousand and up to BGN 5000 thousand		3,0
		1.4.	over BGN 5000 thousand and up to BGN 15000 thousand		3,5
		1.5.	over BGN 15000		4,0
2.	The average number of staff employed	2.1.	up to 50 persons		2,0
		2.2.	between 51 and 100 persons		2,5
		2.3.	between 101 and 500 persons		3,0
		2.4.	between 501 and 1500 persons		3,5
		2.5.	over 1500 persons		4,0
3.	Variation in the operating revenue profitability	3.1.	decline in profitability		-
		3.2.	profitability is maintained		1,0
		3.3.	increase in profitability		2,0
4.	Variation in the financial result	4.1.	maintaining or increasing loss or reduction in profit		-
		4.2.	profit is maintained		1,0
		4.3.	reduction of loss		1,5
		4.4.	increase in profit		2,0
5.	Variation in the added value per employee	5.1.	reduction		-
		5.2.	maintain or increase		2,0
6.	Liabilities of the enterprise	6.1.	non-respected deadlines on current payables and/or irregularly served overdue payables under concluded contracts for their repayment		-
		6.2.	respected deadlines on current payables and regularly served overdue payables under contracts for their repayment		2,0

Source: Annex 2 of https://www.minfin.bg/upload/46760/Implementing+Rules.pdf

In **Chile**, large SOEs are those with sales of over MM USD 54, those with sales between MM USD 54 and MM USD16 for medium-sized SOEs, and those with sales of less than MM USD16 for small SOEs.

In **Colombia**, a calculation method for determining board remuneration is based on the SOE's level of assets, with six different thresholds (see Table 2.3 for details).

In **Costa Rica**, as not all SOEs have the same market size, their net worth is used to evaluate their potential value. Of note, the size of SOEs has not impact on board remuneration.

In **Croatia** and the **Netherlands**, with regard to the remuneration policy, there is no classification of SOEs based on size or sector.

In the **Czech Republic**, while there is no specific regulation defining SOEs according to their size, the *Accounting Act* defines entities in general as follows:

- A small entity should not exceed at least two of these thresholds at the balance sheet date:
  - total assets of CZK 1 000 000 (Czech koruna)
  - annual total net turnover of CZK 200 000 000
  - average number of employees during the accounting period of 50.
- A medium-sized entity should not exceed at least two of these thresholds at the balance sheet date:
  - total assets of CZK 500 000 000
  - annual total net turnover of CZK 1 000 000 000

- ○ average number of employees during the accounting period of 250.
  - A large entity should exceed more than two of the thresholds set for medium-sized entities at the balance sheet date.

In **Estonia**, large SOEs are those with assets over EUR 100 million, those with assets between EUR 10 million and 100 million for medium-sized SOEs, and those with assets below EUR 10 million for small SOEs.

In **Finland**, large companies are either publicly listed companies, or not listed but are in an international business. Small and medium-sized companies are those in a domestic business.

In **Greece**, according to *Law 4308/2014 on Greek accounting standards* in accordance with EU Directive 34/2013, entities are categorised on the basis of their size as follows:

- Micro entities are entities which, at the balance sheet date, do not exceed the limits of at least two of the following three criteria: a) Total assets: EUR 350 000. b) Net turnover: EUR 700 000. c) Average number of employees during the reporting period: ten people.
- Small entities are entities which, at the balance sheet date, do not exceed the limits of two of the following three criteria: a) Total assets: EUR 4 000 000. b) Net turnover: EUR 8 000 000. c) Average number of employees during the reporting period: 50 people.
- Medium entities are entities that are not micro entities or small entities, and which at the balance sheet date do not exceed the limits of two of the following three criteria: a) Total assets: EUR 20 000 000, b) Net turnover: EUR 40 000 000, c) Average number of employees during the reporting period: 250 people.
- Large entities are entities which, at the balance sheet date, exceed the limits of at least two of the following three criteria: a) Total assets: EUR 20 000 000. b) Net turnover: EUR 40 000 000. c) Average number of employees during the reporting period: 250 people.

In **Iceland**, size is determined based on the number of employees, income and total assets.

In **Ireland**, state boards are broken down into four categories for the purposes of determining fee levels. The only determinant of the categorisation is the remuneration of the CEO versus four different civil service levels respective remuneration.

Table A A.1. Fees payable to chairpersons and members of state bodies in Ireland

	Board position	Non-commercial state-sponsored bodies	Commercial state-sponsored bodies
Category 1	Chair	EUR 29 888	EUR 31 500
	Member	EUR 14 963	EUR 15 750
Category 2	Chair	EUR 20 520	EUR 21 600
	Member	EUR 11 970	EUR 12 600
Category 3	Chair	EUR 11 970	EUR 12 600
	Member	EUR 7 695	EUR 8 100
Category 4	Chair	EUR 8 978	EUR 9 450
	Member	EUR 5 985	EUR 6 300

Note: The amounts have been in effect since 1 January 2010, and have remained static since.
Source: https://www.gov.ie/pdf/?file=https://assets.gov.ie/138935/ff9aaf12-0a03-4158-bebe-836bcb1c77e5.pdf#page=null

In **Israel**, the government Companies Authority has established a committee that is in charge of reviewing the classification of state-owned companies, which is reviewed every five years. According to the decision of the committee, the companies are classified according to the size of the company from a score of 1 (lowest) to 10 (highest), according to the following considerations:

- The financial statements, scope of financial balance, income, number of employees, net profit.
- Complexity of the company: activity under market conditions and competition, number of educated employees within the company, number of areas of activity, number of branches, geographical distribution, reporting to the stock exchange or other shareholders.

In **Latvia**, small SOEs may not exceed two of the following criteria: i) assets equal to EUR 4 million, ii) turnover equal to EUR 8 million, iii) 50 employees. Medium-sized SOEs may not exceed two of the following criteria: i) assets equal to EUR 20 million, ii) turnover equal to EUR 40 million, iii) 250 employees. Large SOEs must exceed two of the following criteria: i) assets equal to EUR 20 million, ii) turnover equal to EUR 40 million, iii) 250 employees.

In **Korea**, there are no official criteria/threshold for classifying SOEs as large, small and medium-sized enterprises. In general, most market-type public corporations could be considered large SOEs and quasi-market type public corporations could be considered small or medium-sized corporations, although this is not always the case.

In **Lithuania**, small SOEs may not exceed two of the following criteria: i) sales revenue equal to EUR 8 million, ii) total assets equal to EUR 4 million, iii) 50 employees. Medium-sized SOEs may not exceed two of the following criteria: i) sales revenue equal to EUR 40 million, ii) total assets equal to EUR 20 million, iii) 250 employees. Large SOEs must exceed two of the following criteria: i) sales revenue equal to EUR 40 million, ii) total assets equal to EUR 20 million, iii) 250 employees.

Box A.1. Lithuania's provisions regulating the remuneration of CEOs and deputy directors of statutory SOEs

According to the provisions of the *Remuneration Resolution* (Resolution No. 1 341 of 2002), the monthly salary of executives consists of a fixed and variable part. The fixed part of the monthly salary is determined by the company's category and a respective coefficient assigned to the company. The company's category is determined by the sales figures of the previous year and the average number of employees or total assets, and the coefficient is assigned according to the established category (decision on the specific coefficient is taken by the responsible body – shareholders or board). Coefficients are established on the basis of the basic official salary level set by the Parliament of the Republic of Lithuania to state politicians, judges, state officials and civil servants of the Republic of Lithuania. Of note, if the company has a status of strategic importance for national security, its coefficient for the fixed part of the monthly salary can be increased by up to 75% (on the decision of the body establishing remuneration of the executives of SOEs).

According to the *Remuneration Resolution*, the variable part of the monthly salary of an SOE executive manager cannot exceed 50% of the fixed part. Executive managers are also eligible for annual bonuses from the profit of the enterprise, whose amount cannot exceed the amount of four fixed parts of his/her monthly salary, or a bonus from the savings intended for salaries, which cannot exceed the amount of one fixed part of his/her monthly salary.

Although the remuneration of the executives of state-owned limited liability companies is not regulated, many of these SOEs follow the principles set in the *Remuneration Resolution*. For those who decided not to follow the provisions of the *Resolution*, remuneration usually comprises a fixed monthly salary and a variable component, which can be paid as monthly instalments or as an annual bonus.

Source: Country response to the OECD questionnaire.

In **Norway**, while companies are not classified according to size, the *Norwegian Accounting Act* applies the following definitions:

- § 1-5. Large enterprises shall mean:
  - public limited companies;
  - reporting entities, the shares, units, primary capital certificates or bonds of which are listed on a securities exchange, authorised market place or corresponding regulated market abroad; or
  - other reporting entities if stipulated in regulations laid down by the Ministry.
- § 1-6. Small enterprises shall mean:
  - reporting entities that do not fall within the scope of § 1-5, and that do not exceed two of the three following thresholds as per the balance sheet date: i) sales revenues: 70 million kroner; ii) balance sheet total: 35 million kroner; iii) average number of employees over the financial year: 50.

The *Accounting Act* does not provide a definition for the companies that do not fall under the scope of the above definitions, i.e. which are neither "large" nor "small". For the sake of this report, such companies are defined as medium-sized.

In **Portugal**, SOEs are classified into one of three groups (A, B and C) based on the application of the following indicators: contribution of the public financial effort to the operating result, number of employees, net assets, and turnover. The remuneration amounts of non-executive directors and executive managers of SOEs according to their classification are provided below.

Table A A.2. Remuneration levels of non-executive directors of SOEs in Portugal

Maximum annual remuneration levels (indicated in EUR)

SOE categories	Chair	Vice-chair	Ordinary member
Non-executive members (***without*** participation in a specific committee)			
Group A	20 089.72	18 080.72	16 071.86
Group B	17 076.22	15 368.64	13 661,06
Group C	16 071.86	14 464.66	12 857,46
Non-executive members (***with*** participation in a specific committee)			
Group A	26 786.34	24 107.72	21 429,10
Group B	22 768.34	20 491.52	18 214,70
Group C	21 429.10	19 286.12	17 143,28

Source: Country response to the OECD questionnaire.

Table A A.3. Remuneration levels of executive managers of SOEs in Portugal

Maximum annual remuneration levels (indicated in EUR)

SOE categories	Chair	Vice-chair	Ordinary member
Non-executive members (***without*** participation in a specific committee)			
Group A	20 089.72	18 080.72	16 071.86
Group B	17 076.22	15 368.64	13 661.06
Group C	16 071.86	14 464.66	12 857.46
Non-executive members (***with*** participation in a specific committee)			
Group A	26 786.34	24 107.72	21 429.10

Group B	22 768.34	20 491.52	18 214.70
Group C	21 429.10	19 286.12	17 143.28

Source: Country response to the OECD questionnaire.

In the **Philippines**, the remuneration of SOE governing boards is based on a classification scheme anchored on their assets and revenues.

Table A A.4. Classification of GOCC according to their total amount of assets and revenues

Indicated in PHP (Philippines pesos)

Classification	Assets (PHP)	Revenues (PHP)
A	≥ 100 Billion	≥ 10 Billion
B	≥ 25 Billion and < 100 Billion	≥ 2.5 Billion and > 10 Billion
C	≥ 5 Billion and < 25 Billion	≥ 500 million and < 2.5 Billion
D	≥ 1 Billion and < 5 Billion	≥ 100 million and < 500 million
E	< 1 Billion	< 100 million

Source: Country response to the OECD questionnaire.

Table A A.5. Maximum allowable allowances per meeting and per year (according to GOCC classification)

Indicated in PHP

Classification	Board meetings (PHP)		Committee meetings (PHP)	
	Max per meeting	Max per year	Max per meeting	Max per year
A	40 000	960 000	24 000	576 000
B	20 000	480 000	12 000	288 000
C	15 000	360 000	9 000	216 000
D	10 000	240 000	6 000	144 00
E	5 000	120 000	3 000	72 000

Source: Country response to the OECD questionnaire.

Table A A.6. Actual annual average remuneration of an individual board member (according to GOCC classification)

Indicated in PHP

Classification	Board meetings (PHP)	Committee meetings (PHP)	Performance-based incentives (PHP)	Total remuneration (PHP)
A	960 000	576 000	512 000	2 048 000
B	480 000	288 000	256 000	1 024 000
C	360 000	216 000	192 000	768 000
D	240 000	144 00	128 000	512 00
E	120 000	72 000	64 000	256 000

Source: Country response to the OECD questionnaire.

Annex B. Actual remuneration levels of supervisory board members according SOEs' orientation and size

Actual remuneration levels of supervisory board members (or non-executive directors)

Table A B.1. Average annual remuneration of supervisory board members of commercially oriented SOEs

Shown in actual USD, and (as a percentage of average annual wages)

Country	Board chair				Board vice chair				Ordinary board member			
	Large SOEs	Medium SOEs	Small SOEs	Average total	Large SOEs	Medium SOEs	Small SOEs	Average total	Large SOEs	Medium SOEs	Small SOEs	Average Total
Austria	35 444 (67%)	N/A	N/A		29 536 (56%)	N/A	N/A		23 629 (44%)	N/A	N/A	
Brazil[1]	9 694 (162%)	N/A	6 688 (112%)	9 148 (153%)	9 694 (162%)	N/A	6 688 (112%)	9 148 (153%)	9 694 (162%)	N/A	6 688 (112%)	9 148 (153%)
Bulgaria	28 610 (345%)	N/A	20 211 (244%)	25 250 (304%)	N/A	N/A	N/A	N/A				
Chile[2]	67 418 (252%)	46 467 (174%)	48 271 (181%)	54 052 (202%)	39 234 (147%)	27 511 (103%)	27 344 (102%)	31 363 (117%)	37 649 (141%)	24 660 (92%)	25 205 (94%)	29 171 (109%)
Costa Rica	N/A	N/A	N/A	N/A	10 854 (97%)	16 152 (145%)	10 337 (93%)	12 448 (112%)	10 854 (97%)	16 152 (145%)	10 337 (93%)	12 448 (145%)

Country	Board chair				Board vice chair				Ordinary board member			
	Large SOEs	Medium SOEs	Small SOEs	Average total	Large SOEs	Medium SOEs	Small SOEs	Average total	Large SOEs	Medium SOEs	Small SOEs	Average Total
Croatia	3 780 (23%)	3 780 (23%)	3 780 (23%)	3 780 (23%)	3 780 (23%)	3 780 (23%)	3 780 (23%)	3 780 (23%)	3 780 (23%)	3 780 (23%)	3 780 (23%)	3 780 (23%)
Czech Republic[3]	28 987 (97%)	19 154 (64%)	9 880 (33%)	19 340 (65%)	22 370 (75%)	14 168 (47%)	8 528 (29%)	15 007 (50%)	20 273 (68%)	10 859 (36%)	7 690 (26%)	12 955 (43%)
Estonia[4]	22 020 (72%)	12 760 (42%)		17 390 (57%)	N/A	N/A	N/A	N/A	10 699 (35%)	6 557 (21%)		9 215 (30%)
Finland				34 498 (75%)								20 849 (45%)
France[5]	N/A	N/A	N/A	94 518 (207%)	N/A	N/A	N/A	26 630 (58%)	N/A	N/A	N/A	26 630 (58%)
Iceland	56 235 (83%)	27 992 (41%)	16 678 (25%)	27 414 (41%)	35 629 (54%)	13 945 (21%)	8 279 (12%)	15 164 (22%)	30 539 (45%)	13 945 (21%)	8 279 (12%)	12 020 (18%)
Ireland				19 560 (40%)								11 126 (22%)
Korea	N/A	N/A	N/A	N/A	N/A	N/A	N/A	N/A	N/A	N/A	N/A	23 487 (56%)
Latvia	41 852 (140%)	35 385 (118%)	N/A	38 619 (129%)	39 804 (133%)	N/A	N/A	39 804 (133%)	37 668 (126%)	31 852 (107%)	N/A	34 760 (116%)
Lithuania[6]	24 125 (76%)	15 299 (48%)	11 650 (37%)	18 241 (57%)	N/A	N/A	N/A	N/A	16 829 (53%)	9 768 (62%)	3 884 (12%)	10 592 (33%)
Netherlands[6]	52 279 (8%)	43 184 (73%)	22 962 (39%)	44 873 (76%)	38 641 (66%)	31 252 (53%)		34 946 (59%)	38 641 (66%)	30 691 (52%)	18 756 (33%)	26 696 (45%)
New Zealand	67 594 (149%)	47 576 (105%)	30 315 (67%)	48 520 (107%)	42 312 (93%)	29 761 (66%)	18 963 (42%)	30 345 (67%)	33 854 (75%)	23 803 (53%)	15 168 (34%)	24 275 (54%)
Norway	50 166 (90%)	37 639 (67%)	25 330 (45%)	38 555 (69%)	32 159 (58%)	21 574 (39%)	12 519 (22%)	23 410 (42%)	26 463 (47%)	18 219 (33%)	14 353 (23%)	19 341 (35%)

Country	Board chair				Board vice chair				Ordinary board member			
	Large SOEs	Medium SOEs	Small SOEs	Average total	Large SOEs	Medium SOEs	Small SOEs	Average total	Large SOEs	Medium SOEs	Small SOEs	Average Total
Portugal[7]	31 331 (110%)	26 631 (94%)	25 065 (88%)	27 673 (97%)	28 206 (99%)	23 977 (84%)	22 568 (79%)	24 919 (88%)	25 076 (88%)	21 314 (75%)	20 060 (71%)	22 150 (78%)
Slovak Republic[8]	9 767 (41%)	3 635 (15%)	8 872 (38%)	7 712 (33%)	10 073 (43%)	N/A	N/A	10 073 (43%)	6 728 (28%)	2 631 (11%)	6 193 (26%)	5 184 (22%)
Sweden	56 879 (121%)	35 622 (76%)	17 811 (38%)	36 196 (77%)	N/A	N/A	N/A	N/A	26 429 (56%)	17 236 (37%)	8 732 (19%)	17 121 (36%)
Turkey				16 150 (273%)				8 075 (137%)				8 075 (137%)

Note: Data covers non-listed SOEs with a state shareholding of at least 50% which are not listed on the stock exchange, except for **Chile** where data includes one listed SOE (ZOFRI), albeit with remuneration levels similar to those of non-listed SOEs.

Data unavailable for **Australia, Belgium, Colombia, Germany, Greece, Hungary, Israel, Japan, Mexico, Peru, Philippines** and **Spain**. Data partially available for **Bulgaria, Chile, France, Korea, Lithuania** and the **Netherlands**. For details on SOE classification according to orientation and size, see Annex A.

[1] In **Brazil**, SOEs are classified as "dependent" and "non-dependent".

[2] For **Chile**, indicated amounts refer to the maximum remuneration levels for each board member (as opposed to the average), and include performance-related compensation.

[3] In the **Czech Republic**, SOEs are divided between commercial companies and state enterprises.

[4] In **Estonia**, SOE boards do not include a "vice chair" position.

[5] In **France**, SOEs are not categorised according to their commercial or public policy orientation.

[6] In **Lithuania** and the **Netherlands**, indicated amounts refer to all SOEs regardless of their orientation. In the **Netherlands**, SOEs include BNG, COVRA, FMO, Gasunie, Holland Casino, Invest NL, Nederlandse Loterij, NIO, NS, Schipol, SRH, TenneT, UCN.

[7] For **Portugal**, indicated amounts refer to the maximum remuneration levels for each board member (as opposed to the average), and to all SOEs regardless of their orientation.

[8] For the **Slovak Republic**, indicated amounts refer to remuneration levels of board members of SOEs operating only in the transportation sector.

Source: Country responses to the OECD questionnaire supplemented by desk research, and OECD calculations based on OECD database (https://data.oecd.org/earnwage/average-wages.htm) and ILOSTAT database (https://ilostat.ilo.org/topics/wages/).

Table A B.2. Average annual remuneration of supervisory board members of public policy-oriented SOEs

Shown in actual USD, and (as a percentage of average annual wages)

Country	Board chair				Board vice chair				Ordinary board member			
	Large SOEs	Medium SOEs	Small SOEs	Average total	Large SOEs	Medium SOEs	Small SOEs	Average total	Large SOEs	Medium SOEs	Small SOEs	Average Total
Austria	3 072 (6%)	2 835 (5%)	2 126 (4%)	2 835 (5%)	2 835 (5%)	2 600 (5%)	2 000 (4%)	2 600 (5%)	2 363 (4%)	2 362 (4%)	1 890 (4%)	2 363 (4%)
Brazil[1]	7 233 (121%)	N/A	7 284 (122%)	7 261 (121%)	7 233 (121%)	N/A	7 284 (122%)	7 261 (121%)	7 233 (121%)	N/A	7 284 (122%)	7 261 (121%)
Bulgaria		N/A			N/A	N/A	N/A	N/A	20 512 (247%)	20 049 (242%)	16 944 (204%)	19 169 (123%)
Costa Rica[2]	N/A	N/A	N/A	N/A	6 246 (56%)	4 941 (44%)	2 169 (19%)	4 452 (40%)	6 246 (56%)	4 941 (44%)	2 169 (19%)	4 452 (40%)
Croatia	3 780 (23%)	3 780 (23%)	3 780 (23%)	3 780 (23%)	3 780 (23%)	3 780 (23%)	3 780 (23%)	3 780 (23%)	3 780 (23%)	3 780 (23%)	3 780 (23%)	3 780 (23%)
Czech Republic[3]	13 888 (46%)	3 961 (12%)	2 889 (10%)	6 897 (23%)	9 786 (33%)	2 330 (8%)	2 377 (8%)	4 847 (16%)	7 643 (26%)	2 330 (8%)	2 330 (8%)	4 101 (14%)
Estonia[4]	15 183 (49%)	12 311 (40%)	6 530 (21%)	11 150 (36%)	N/A	N/A	N/A	N/A	7 827 (25%)	6 532 (21%)	3 646 (12%)	5 911 (19%)
Finland		N/A		34 498 (75%)								
Iceland	38 853 (58%)	24 925 (37%)	13 670 (20%)	18 204 (27%)	29 026 (43%)	12 606 (19%)	5 790 (9%)	9 431 (14%)	19 347 (29%)	12 606 (19%)	5 790 (9%)	8 626 (13%)
Ireland				18 573 (38%)								10 568 (21%)
Latvia	34 934 (117%)		12 854 (43%)	23 894 (80%)	N/A	N/A	N/A	N/A	29 740 (100%)		11 041 (37%)	20 391 (68%)

Country	Board chair				Board vice chair				Ordinary board member			
	Large SOEs	Medium SOEs	Small SOEs	Average total	Large SOEs	Medium SOEs	Small SOEs	Average total	Large SOEs	Medium SOEs	Small SOEs	Average Total
New Zealand	48 703 (108%)	34 575 (76%)	32 175 (71%)	38 484 (85%)	31 928 (71%)	21 605 (48%)	20 103 (44%)	24 545 (54%)	24 105 (53%)	17 617 (39%)	16 082 (36%)	19 268 (43%)
Norway		26 365 (47%)		26 365 (47%)		15 573 (28%)		15 573 (28%)		14 961 (27%)		14 961 (27%)
Slovak Republic[5]	10 203 (43%)			10 203 (43%)	10 790 (46%)	N/A	N/A	10 790 (46%)	6 917 (29%)			6 917 (29%)
Turkey				16 150 (273%)				8 075 (137%)				8 075 (137%)

Note: Data covers SOEs with a state shareholding of at least 50% which are not listed on the stock exchange, except for **Chile** where data includes one listed SOE (ZOFRI), albeit with remuneration levels similar to those of non-listed SOEs.

In **France, Lithuania,** the **Netherlands** and **Portugal,** SOEs are not classified according to their orientation. Data unavailable for **Australia, Belgium, Colombia, Germany, Greece, Hungary, Israel, Japan, Korea, Mexico, Peru, Philippines** and **Spain.** Data partially available for **Bulgaria.** For details on SOE classification according to orientation and size, see Annex A.

[1] In **Brazil,** SOEs are classified as "dependent" and "non-dependent".

[2] In **Costa Rica,** the chair of the board is the CEO.

[3] In the **Czech Republic,** SOEs are divided between commercial companies and state enterprises.

[4] In **Estonia,** SOE boards do not include a "vice chair" position.

[5] For the **Slovak Republic,** indicated amounts refer to remuneration levels of board members of SOEs operating only in the transportation sector.

Source: Country responses to the OECD questionnaire supplemented by desk research, and OECD calculations based on OECD database (https://data.oecd.org/earnwage/average-wages.htm) and ILOSTAT database (https://ilostat.ilo.org/topics/wages/).

Annex C. Actual remuneration levels of executive managers according to SOEs' orientation and size

Table A C.1. Average annual remuneration of executive managers of commercially oriented SOEs (in actual USD and as a multiple of average wages)

Shown in actual USD, and (as a multiple of average annual wages)

Country	Chief Executive Officer (CEO)				Chief Financial Officer (CFO)				Chief Operating Officer (COO)			
	Large SOEs	Medium SOEs	Small SOEs	Average total	Large SOEs	Medium SOEs	Small SOEs	Average total	Large SOEs	Medium SOEs	Small SOEs	Average Total
Austria	586 400 (11)	N/A	164 192 (3.1)	375 296 (7.1)								
Brazil[1]	117 724	N/A	66 696	108 446 (19)	108 848	N/A	62 400	100 402	108 848	N/A	62 400	100 402
Bulgaria	63 120	43 607	32 084	46 270 (5.5)								
Chile[2]	250 000 (9.3)	231 000	142 500	207 833 (7.8)	226 761	108 482	81 678	138 973	229 857	121 941	83 966	145 255
Costa Rica[3]	128 551	125 310	53 340	102 400 (9.2)	125 892	107 490	34 094	89 159	476 929	113 178	36 106	208 738
Croatia[4]				46 824 (2.8)								
Estonia	197 303	84 977	N/A	141 075 (4.6)	178 078	N/A	N/A	178 078	159 098	48 161	N/A	103 606
Finland	N/A	N/A	N/A	404 657 (8.7)	N/A	N/A	N/A	N/A	N/A	N/A	N/A	N/A

Country	Chief Executive Officer (CEO)				Chief Financial Officer (CFO)				Chief Operating Officer (COO)			
	Large SOEs	Medium SOEs	Small SOEs	Average total	Large SOEs	Medium SOEs	Small SOEs	Average total	Large SOEs	Medium SOEs	Small SOEs	Average Total
France[5]				351 600 (7.7)								
Iceland	325 840	179 320	152 363	200 416 (2.9)								
Ireland	283 869	208 330	182 289	224 829 (4.5)								
Korea[6]				182 274 (4.3)								
Latvia[7]	170 451	112 973		141 712 (4.7)	N/A	N/A	N/A	N/A	153 367	101 643	N/A	127 478
Lithuania[8]	136 597	69 704	55 646	75 493 (2.4)								
Netherlands[9]	414 000	370 000	194 000	326 000 (5.5)	399 000	309 000	N/A	354 000				
New Zealand[10]	621 437	445 800	246 027	437 755 (9.6)	N/A	N/A	N/A	M/A	N/A	N/A	N/A	N/A
Norway	511 675	282 896	188 719	318 362 (5.7)	N/A	N/A	N/A	N/A	N/A	N/A	N/A	N/A
Peru[11]	N/A	N/A	N/A	106 667 (18.7)	N/A	N/A	N/A	88 000	N/A	N/A	N/A	80 000
Portugal[12]	126 494	107 520	101 212	111 737 (3.9)	113 838	96 762	91 070	102 900	101 182	86 004	80 945	89 377
Slovak Republic	124 085	56 091	51 294	77 159 (3.2)	109 646	N/A	45 256	77 452	90 776	41 395	32 420	65 928
Sweden	684 776	381 819	210 105	425 567 (9.4)	N/A	N/A	N/A	N/A	N/A	N/A	N/A	N/A
Turkey[13]				23 675 (4)								

Notes: Data covers executive remuneration of non-listed SOEs with a state shareholding of at least 50% which are not listed on the stock exchange, except for **Chile** where data includes one listed SOE (ZOFRI), albeit with remuneration levels similar to those of non-listed SOEs.
Data includes fixed remuneration only, except for **Brazil, Estonia, Finland, Latvia**, the **Netherlands** and **New Zealand** where both fixed and variable remuneration are included.

Data unavailable for **Australia, Belgium, Colombia**, the **Czech Republic, Germany, Greece, Hungary, Israel, Japan, Philippines, Portugal, Spain, Switzerland** and the **United Kingdom**. Data partially available for **Bulgaria, Iceland, New Zealand, Norway** and **Sweden**.

[1] In **Brazil**, SOEs are classified as "dependent" and "non-dependent". Indicated amounts refer to total average annual remuneration, including both fixed and variable components.

[2] For **Chile**, data includes average remuneration levels in all SOEs, regardless of their orientation.

[3] In **Costa Rica**, large SOEs include ICE and INS; medium-sized SOEs include NBCR, BCR, JAPDEVA; small SOEs include CR Mail Service, INCOP, SINART.

[4] Indicated amount for **Croatia** refers to the net salary paid to executive managers in legal entities of special interest to the Republic of Croatia in December 2020.

[5] In **France**, the indicated amount refers to the average annual remuneration of CEOs of all SOEs, regardless of their orientation.

[6] In **Korea**, the indicated amount refers to the average remuneration of the CEO of public corporations for 2020. For market-type public corporations, the average remuneration of the CEO for 2020 amounted to KRW 229 519 000 (Korean won) (equivalent to USD 194 775), and for quasi-market type public corporations for the same period, it amounted to KRW 204 321 000 (equivalent to USD 173 125).

[7] In **Latvia**, indicated amounts refer to the remuneration levels paid to, respectively, the CEO, the CFO/COO (same amount), and ordinary executive board members.

[8] In **Lithuania**, indicated amounts refer to the average annual remuneration of CEOs of all SOEs, regardless of their orientation.

[9] In the **Netherlands**, indicated amounts refer to the average annual remuneration of CEOs of all SOEs, regardless of their orientation. Large SOEs include Air France/KLM, BNG, NS, NWB Bank, TenneT. Medium-sized SOEs include GasUnie, Havenbedrijf Rotterdam, Holland Casino, Nederlandse Loterij, Schiphol, Thales. Small SOEs include COVRA, FMO, Invest NL, NIO, SRH, UCN.

[10] In **New Zealand**, large commercially oriented SOEs include those with annual revenue above NZD 4 000 million; medium-sized commercially oriented SOEs, those with annual revenue above NZD 800 million; and small commercially oriented SOEs, those with annual revenue below NZD 50 million.

[11] In **Peru**, the SOEs under the scope of FONFAE are all considered commercially oriented.

[12] In **Portugal**, indicated amounts refer to the remuneration levels paid to, respectively, the president, the vice president, and ordinary executive board members of all SOEs, regardless of their orientation.

[13] In **Turkey**, the indicated amount refer to the average annual fee based on the upper limits of director generals according January 2021 data.

Source: Country responses to the OECD questionnaire supplemented by desk research, and OECD calculations based on OECD database (https://data.oecd.org/earnwage/average-wages.htm) and ILOSTAT database (https://ilostat.ilo.org/topics/wages/).

Table A C.2. Average annual remuneration of executive managers of public policy-oriented SOEs (in actual USD and as a multiple of average wages)

Shown in actual USD, and (as a multiple of average annual wages)

Country	Chief Executive Officer (CEO)				Chief Financial Officer (CFO)				Chief Operating Officer (COO)			
	Large SOEs	Medium SOEs	Small SOEs	Average total	Large SOEs	Medium SOEs	Small SOEs	Average total	Large SOEs	Medium SOEs	Small SOEs	Average Total
Austria	328 143	257 827	164 072	250 015 (4.7)								
Brazil[1]	70 840	N/A	68 548	69 550 (11.6)	68 857	N/A	65 673	67 066	68 857	N/A	65 673	67 066
Bulgaria	52 315	40 441	34 405	40 609 (4.9)								
Costa Rica[2]	56 188	39 018	53 295	49 500 (4.4)	45 023	37 795	44 126	42 315	44 508	33 276	N/A	38 892

Country	Chief Executive Officer (CEO)				Chief Financial Officer (CFO)				Chief Operating Officer (COO)			
	Large SOEs	Medium SOEs	Small SOEs	Average total	Large SOEs	Medium SOEs	Small SOEs	Average total	Large SOEs	Medium SOEs	Small SOEs	Average Total
Croatia[3]				46 824 (2.8)								
Estonia	144 287	94 703	65 500	99 357 (3.2)	133 065	70 389	N/A	117 396	114 649	83 138	49 297	95 508
Finland				324 124 (7)								
Iceland	201 581	150 014	147 670	153 530 (2.3)								
Ireland	197 892	161 348	122 381	160 540 (3.2)								
Korea[4]				156 628 (3.7)								
Latvia[5]	102 445	82 619	52 388	79 151 (2.6)	N/A	N/A	N/A	N/A	87 042	70 568	48 832	68 805
New Zealand[6]	369 936	264 700	274 751	303 129 (6.7)	N/A	N/A	N/A	N/A	N/A	N/A	N/A	N/A
Norway	N/A	224 520	102 499	215 452 (3.8)	N/A	N/A	N/A	N/A	N/A	N/A	N/A	N/A
Slovak Republic	89 702	N/A	N/A	89 702 (3.8)	91 642	N/A	N/A	91 642	97 085	N/A	N/A	97 085
Turkey[7]				23 675 (4)								

Notes: Data covers executive remuneration of non-listed SOEs with a state shareholding of at least 50% which are not listed on the stock exchange, except for **Chile** where data includes one listed SOE (ZOFRI), albeit with remuneration levels similar to those of non-listed SOEs.

Data includes fixed remuneration only, except for **Brazil**, **Estonia**, **Finland**, **Latvia**, the **Netherlands** and **New Zealand**.

Data unavailable for **Australia**, **Belgium**, **Colombia**, the **Czech Republic**, **France**, **Germany**, **Greece**, **Hungary**, **Israel**, **Japan**, **Peru**, **Philippines**, **Spain**, **Sweden**, **Switzerland** and the **United Kingdom**. Data partially available for **Bulgaria**, **Iceland**, **New Zealand** and **Norway**. Data for **France**, **Lithuania**, the **Netherlands** and **Portugal** are reported in Table B.3 above. For **Chile**, data is available regardless of SOE orientation, and as such remuneration levels in all SOEs are reported in Table B.3 above.

[1] In **Brazil**, SOEs are classified as "dependent" and "non-dependent". Indicated amounts refer to total average annual remuneration, including both fixed and variable components.

[2] In **Costa Rica**, large SOEs include AYA; medium-sized SOEs include INCOFER, JPS, RECOPE; and small SOEs include CNP.

[3] The indicated amount for **Croatia** refers to the net salary paid to executive managers in legal entities of special interest to the Republic of Croatia in December 2020.

[4] In **Korea**, the indicated amount refers to the average remuneration of the CEO of quasi-governmental institutions for 2020. For fund management type quasi-governmental institutions, the average remuneration of the CEO for 2020 amounted to KRW 239 448 000 (equivalent to USD 202 888), and for commissioned service type quasi-governmental institutions for the same period, it amounted to KRW 176 301 000 (equivalent to USD 149 383).

5 In **Latvia**, indicated amounts refer to the remuneration levels paid to, respectively, the CEO, the CFO/COO (slightly differentiated amounts), and ordinary executive board members.

6 In **New Zealand**, large public policy-oriented SOEs include those with annual revenue above NZD 1 600 million; medium-sized public policy-oriented SOEs, those with annual revenue above NZD 250 million; and small public policy-oriented SOEs, those with annual revenue below NZD 30 million.

7 In **Turkey**, the indicated amount refer to the average annual fee based on the upper limits of director generals according January 2021 data.

Source: Country responses to the OECD questionnaire supplemented by desk research, and OECD calculations based on OECD database (https://data.oecd.org/earnwage/average-wages.htm) and ILOSTAT database (https://ilostat.ilo.org/topics/wages/).

www.ingramcontent.com/pod-product-compliance
Lightning Source LLC
Chambersburg PA
CBHW080619270326
41928CB00016B/3130